IT'S A GREAT DAY TO FUND-RAISE!

IT'S A GREAT DAY TO FUND-RAISE!

A Veteran Campaigner Reveals the
Development Tips and Techniques
That Will Work for You

Tony Poderis

FundAmerica Press
Cleveland, Ohio

Printed in the United States of America
Second printing 1998

Pagemaking and design by Kathleen Mills
Cover design by Bill Szilagyi
Cover photograph by Don Krejci
Cover location courtesy of KeyBank

Library of Congress Catalog Card Number: 96-84730
ISBN 0-9652066-0-2 (Hardcover)
ISBN 0-9652066-1-0 (Softcover)

Tony Poderis may be contacted at any of the following addresses:
2901 Istra Lane
Willoughby Hills, Ohio 44092

e-mail: Tony@raise-funds.com
website: www.raise-funds.com
fax: 440-944-6877

Contents

Acknowledgments

This book would not have been possible without the contributions of these individuals, whom I would like to gratefully acknowledge:

George M. Keith, who gave me my first fund-raising job. His mentoring instilled in me many of the concepts of fund-raising which are presented here.

The late **Ralph Black,** who gave me the opportunity and confidence to lead my first fund-raising workshops during his tenure as national workshop director for the American Symphony Orchestra League.

The late **Alfred M. Rankin,** who, as president of the Cleveland Orchestra's board of trustees, hired me as the orchestra's first director of development. His dedication and devotion to that institution was a great inspiration to me.

David Patterson, without whose writing skills and insight it would not have been possible to turn my oral and written workshop presentations into this book.

Diana Tittle, whose publishing expertise kept me on course in the creation of a book whose purpose is to help as many people as possible succeed at fund-raising.

Introduction

Non-profit organizations, no matter what their field of endeavor or size, share a common need for contributed income. They use it to offset operational deficits, build endowment, and enable expansion. Contributed income is the lifeblood of non-profits, and the primary means of acquiring it is the fund-raising campaign.

This book is about fund-raising campaigns. It is also about boards of trustees, individual donors, philanthropic foundations, corporate givers, volunteers, and development professionals. And the thread that ties them all together is the fund-raising campaign—that concerted effort to induce donors to make contributions during a predetermined period of time to a non-profit organization for a specific purpose.

I began my professional fund-raising career as a consultant in the early 1970s. I then spent 20 years as the Cleveland Orchestra's first director of development and more recently have returned to consulting. In the last quarter century, I have managed or consulted on scores of fund-raising campaigns.

When I took part in my first campaign as a volunteer solicitor for the Big Brothers of Greater Cleveland nearly 30 years ago, fund-raising was in its infancy. There was nowhere near the number of non-profits then that there are now, and outside of colleges and universities only a handful employed professionals as development officers.

At the time, I worked for the General Electric Company marketing automotive lamps, and I found that a marketer's skills also made for a successful fund-raiser. In the end, selling light bulbs wasn't all that different a process from convincing someone to give to a worthy cause. What I experienced as a campaign volunteer was the foundation for my career as a professional fund-raising director. In the ensuing years, I have learned a great deal more about fund-raising and the collaborative effort it requires.

This book is an attempt to share that hard-earned knowledge with other fund-raisers. By fund-raiser, I mean anyone who works in any capacity on a fund-raising campaign, and throughout these pages the term fund-raiser is used to refer to volunteers and professionals alike.

This book is for fund-raisers—trustees, campaign leaders, volunteer solicitors, organization staff members, development officers, and consultants alike. It offers a practical, hands-on approach to identifying funding sources, rating and evaluating prospective donors, and planning and managing a campaign. It explores annual, endowment, capital, sponsorship, and underwriting campaigns, examining their similarities and their differences.

You will learn how to create and articulate a case for support, develop a realistic campaign goal that balances need against resources, produce a solicitation kit, structure a campaign, assess results, and—most important of all—ask for the money. Along the way, we will examine the roles of trustees, development professionals, consultants, and volunteers in a campaign, and as members of the development team.

This book will show you how to increase your organization's funding, broaden its community support, and promote greater volunteer involvement. It answers the questions I have seen crop up over and over again in nearly three decades of experience as a fund-raiser.

Perhaps the most often voiced of those questions is, "When is the best time to ask for money?" The answer is TODAY. Never mind waiting for the economy to improve, for the holidays to be over, for summer to end, or any of the other excuses we give for holding back.

Every day is a great day to fund-raise, so let's begin today!

CHAPTER 1

The Truths,
The Whole Truths,
And Nothing But The Truths

Conventional wisdom tells us fund-raising is impossible and that the process is something of a mystery. (Just ask anyone who has failed at it or has managed to avoid being held accountable for it.)

Everybody knows you need a proven track record if you are to successfully raise money. (Just look at all the help-wanted ads for development officers that list as a qualification "successful history of managing a major annual campaign or soliciting large donations.")

It's common knowledge that corporations and foundations give most of the money. (Just ask anyone who has never done any fund-raising or who would find a contribution of $100 a strain on the family budget.)

Those three "facts" of development are among the misconceptions that have helped doom many a fund-raising campaign, and when it comes to misconceptions, fund-raising has more than its share of them. Whenever anyone offering fund-raising advice touts that advice as the conventional wisdom, or what everybody knows, or as common knowledge, run. Do not pass Go. Do not stop to collect $200. Run.

On the other hand, there are some insights about fund-raising which successful fund-raisers have gained. These insights often fly in the face of conventional wisdom. They neither offer shortcuts nor promise instant results. However, they are not hard to understand, and nearly anyone can profit from them. They are:

The Nine Basic Truths of Fund-Raising

BT 1: **Organizations are not entitled to support; they must earn it.**

No matter what an organization's good works, it must prove to those who support it the value of those works to the community and the efficiency with which the organization delivers them. The primary key to fund-raising success is to have a first-class organization in every sense. There are no entitlements in the non-profit world.

BT 2: **Successful fund-raising is not magic; it is simply hard work on the part of people who are thoroughly prepared.**

There are no magic wands, spells, or incantations. Whenever you hear that someone has the magic fund-raising touch, laugh. Otherwise the joke is likely to be on you. No one pulls a rabbit—complete with its own lettuce farm—out of the fund-raising hat. No one! Fund-raising is simple in design and concept, but it is very hard work! It is planning, executing, and assessing. It is paying attention to detail. It is knowing your organization and what it needs. It is knowing who has the money and how much they can give.

BT 3: **Fund-raising is not raising money; it is raising friends.**

People who do not like you do not give to you. People who know little about your organization give little at best. Only those people who know and like you will support you. Raise friends and you will raise money.

BT 4: **You do not raise money by begging for it; you raise it by selling people on your organization.**

No matter how good your organization, how valuable its services, how efficiently it delivers them, people will not give money unless they are convinced to do so. Fund-raisers function much as sales and marketing people do in the commercial world.

BT 5: **People do not just reach for their checkbooks and give money to an organization; they have to be asked to give.**

No matter how well you sell people on your organization, no matter how much money they have, no matter how capable they are of giving it, they have to be asked for it. People with money to give are accustomed to being asked for it. The worst thing that will happen to you is that they will say no, and even then they are likely to be supportive, even apologetic.

BT 6: **You don't wait for the "right" moment to ask; you ask now.**

If you are always looking for the right moment to ask for the money, you will never find it. You have to be ready, willing, and able to close the sale. You have to take the risk of hearing no. If that happens, don't take the rejection to heart. The person is saying no to the organization, not to you. Once you have presented your case ask for the money, either close the sale, find out what the objection to giving is and overcome it, or get your turndown and move on.

BT 7: **Successful fund-raising officers do not ask for money; they get others to ask for it.**

The professional fund-raising officer is the last person who should ask prospects for money. The request should come from someone within a prospect's peer group. It is the job of the professional development officer to design, put together, and manage the campaign. Volunteers who are themselves business executives, well-off individuals, community leaders, or board members are the ones who should ask their counterparts for donations.

BT 8: **You don't decide today to raise money and then ask for it tomorrow: it takes time, patience, and planning to raise money.**

Make the decision to initiate a fund-raising campaign before the need. It takes time to develop a campaign and its leadership. With each prospective donor the chances are you will get only one chance to present your case; be prepared. If you present a poorly prepared case, you will be told no.

BT 9: **Prospects and donors are not cash crops waiting to be harvested; treat them as you would customers in a business.**

No successful business person deals with customers as if they had a responsibility to buy. Prospects and donors have to be courted as you would court a customer. They must be told how important they are, treated with courtesy and respect, and if you expect to do business with them again, thanked.

There are, of course, exceptions to each of these basic truths, but if you rely on the exception to support your organization you will find incidences of it are few and far between. In the end we raise money from people who have it, can afford to give it, are sold on the benefit of what we are doing, wouldn't have given it to us unless we had asked, and whose gifts are appreciated and respected.

It doesn't take a genius to raise money. The process is a combination of common sense, hard work, preparation, courtesy, commitment, enthusiasm, understanding, and a belief in what you are selling.

The best fund-raising officers manage campaigns. They rarely ask individuals for money. They provide fund-raising plans and tools to others better positioned to do the actual asking. Development officers are facilitators. The money they raise supports their organization's work, but their efforts are best deployed when they are the behind-the-scenes support of others who do the asking.

CHAPTER 2

In the Beginning

All fund-raising campaigns begin with a realization that the organization needs money, usually voiced to the person charged with fund-raising as, "We need to raise \$____." The amount varies, but once accepted it becomes the *Goal*. Whether the effort is to be the regular clockwork of an annual campaign or a one-shot designed to raise money for a specific, non-recurring purpose, it begins and ends with the goal. Success or failure is measured incrementally by how far above or below goal the campaign finishes.

The first step in setting the goal is to look at the resources you plan to tap and see if they can meet the stated need. Even organizations with modest contributed-income needs will find the following example of this principle instructive. Once at a board meeting of the Cleveland Orchestra, an influential and highly respected trustee got up and said, "What we need is more endowment. We ought to have a \$50 million endowment campaign."

In the end the goal we decided on was \$40 million, not \$50 million. An assessment of our prospective donors, even when we put down the greatest amounts we could imagine receiving from our strongest benefactors, showed that \$50 million was too ambitious. This was not a campaign which we had conducted before, and even to raise \$40 million was a formidable challenge.

Would those of us who had the responsibility for managing the campaign rather have had a less intimidating number for our goal? You bet. But how do you tell your boss that something his boss had decided is imperative can't be done? You don't, unless you are absolutely, 100 percent sure and have the evidence to back your argument. Even then the risk is high. Development officers are paid to see to it that the money is raised, not to explain why it can't be raised. So you look for ways to accomplish what you are asked to do, and then determine whether the goal needs to be modified.

In the case of an annual campaign you look at last year's results. Who were the major donors and at what level did they give? How many of them have died or left town? Will the ones who remain give at the same level or higher? Do you have a list of prospects from which to draw new donors? Are there board members and volunteers ready to step forward and lead the campaign this year?

If the campaign—its purpose and plan—has not been executed previously, if it doesn't have a history, you are starting from ground zero, and that's tougher. Will people who have supported your other fund-raising efforts support this campaign with *additional* money? (It does no good to move money from one pocket to another.) Will the purpose of this campaign garner you support from new givers? Again, do you have the volunteer leadership in place to make this campaign a success?

Toughest of all is when your organization has absolutely no demonstrated base of support. We're not talking about launching a new campaign, but about an organization that has never conducted a fund-raising campaign of any kind. Now you must base your assessment, not on your organization's experience, but rather on the ways in which your community has supported other organizations. Most crucial of all, you must assess whether your board can be counted on for fund-raising leadership. Something you have never asked of them before.

Leadership is the key element in determining the goal or deciding whether you should even conduct a campaign. Be it is this year's edition of the annual campaign, a first-time attempt to raise endowment, or a first-ever fund-raising effort, leadership is what will make or break your campaign.

A new arts organization brought me in to design an annual fund-raising campaign that would support its exhibitions. I provided a plan and the tools (we'll talk about plans and tools later in this book) to conduct a successful campaign. The board committed to the concept, even praised it. About halfway through the campaign the board members asked me to come to a meeting. The meeting revolved around the fact that so far in the campaign they had failed to meet their goals. They were going to have to postpone their inaugural exhibition, and they wanted to know what was going wrong.

It was simple. The trustees had talked the talk, but hadn't walked the walk. When left on their own they had proved unready and unwilling to pick up fund-raising tools they had praised and use them to execute a plan they had approved. Each board member was sitting back on his or her heels waiting for someone else to raise the money. All the ingredients were in place except one—leadership. An excellent plan using proven tools in a community known for giving to such causes had failed. In the end, everything hinged on leadership, and that leadership just wasn't there.

In another instance, I was consulted about eight months into a fund-raising campaign for a new building for a social service institution. The organization was well respected, well known, and trying to raise several million dollars. Here, there was a board ready and willing to provide the leadership for a campaign. I was there because the board realized that even with all their commitment they weren't getting the job done. With ground-breaking already eight months behind them, they had only raised $500,000. Time was slipping away; they were losing the impetus and sense of immediacy that a construction project brings to prospective donors. My mission was to pull together a better working plan and provide the tools of a fund-raising campaign. I was being asked to build the engine of a campaign. I did, the board embraced it, raised the money, and finished the building.

In both these campaigns something had gone wrong. The social service organization had a committed leadership but lacked the tools, while the arts organization had all the tools in front of it but had not used them. In both situations the solution was simple. The social service organization's board needed only a workable plan and well-designed tools. The arts organization's board needed to step forward and lead. Once a campaign has begun it is still possible for a development officer or consultant to provide better fund-raising tools, but if there is a failure in leadership the solution must come from within that leadership. The organization's board has to reach into itself and find the will and commitment to lead a campaign.

There is no greater strength in a fund-raising campaign than a board ready and willing to lead. There is no greater weakness than one which sees fund-raising as someone else's responsibility.

So that's where you start the process of a fund-raising campaign—with your board. You have to have their commitment to be fund-raisers and to recruit additional volunteer fund-raisers. (Do your board members have a job description which includes the words, ". . . will lead fund-raising campaigns and actively solicit gifts"?) It is their leadership that will make or break a campaign. They are the ones an organization will draw upon to establish a campaign committee and to make or find lead gifts. When it comes to fund-raising campaigns you need an attainable goal, a plan for getting to that goal, and the tools to execute that plan. But in the end, the success or failure of a fund-raising campaign hinges on leadership, and that leadership starts on your board.

CHAPTER 3

Know Your Organization

You start the process of becoming a fund-raiser for an organization when you first become involved with the organization. That's when you begin to acquire knowledge about an organization, and acquisition of knowledge is the first step in preparing to raise money. To sell any product, it is important to know just what that product is and what it does. It makes no difference whether you are a waitress explaining the intricacies of the specials of the day, a computer salesperson pitching the new improved model, or a solicitor in a fund-raising campaign.

If you are the person running a campaign, you must make sure your solicitors have access to information about what the organization is, what it does, and why money is needed in the furtherance of what goals. If you are the person asking for the money, think about how you would go about making your request without that information. Yes, you will on occasion find people who will give because *you* ask rather than give to the cause, but that is the exception, and—this can't be said often enough—you cannot rely on the exception to support your organization.

New board members should be invited to attend a formal orientation session exposing them to what the organization does, how it is important to the community, why its services are necessary, and what their role will be. Volunteer solicitors in a campaign should be given the same information. Professional development officers need to steep themselves in the workings of the organization from their first day on the job.

No matter what your position or role in an organization's fund-raising efforts, the *mission statement* is the single most important thing you must understand. The mission statement outlines the organization's values and purposes, programs and services, and hopes and dreams—its priorities. Printed on the back of a schedule, gracing the first page of an annual report or emblazoned on a lobby wall, it purports to delineate the whys and wherefores, explain the purpose, and elucidate the value to the community of an organization. It is, or should be, a statement of an organization's reason for being and its strengths. As such it is the first statement in the litany for fund-raising.

You can't make the case for support unless you know your organization's strengths.

Neither can you expect to succeed without an understanding of its weaknesses and perceived negatives. I remember a campaign I worked on during my first year in fund-raising. A hospital was trying to raise money to build a new 200-bed facility to replace its existing 100 beds. Sounds reasonable at first blush. The problem was the hospital only had a 40 percent occupancy rate. Our job was to raise money to add 100 beds to a hospital which already had 60 empty beds. There goes the argument for needed expansion.

However, we understood that seeming weakness in our case and why it existed. As a result, we were able to eliminate the perception of it as a negative argument against our campaign. The hospital was better than half empty because it was antiquated. Doctors didn't want to send their patients there. The solution was to build a new hospital, and the community needed the additional 100 *modern* beds.

My point is this: If your organization has a weakness that can be perceived as a fund-raising negative, you don't ignore it. You face it head on, take the offensive, and turn it into a fund-raising strength.

New and forming organizations are fraught with weaknesses and perceived fund-raising negatives. To begin with, the community got along without them in the past. How does a new organization know it is needed now? Has it done a market analysis? Is there a compelling reason for the organization to exist and for specific people to support it? The answer to those questions can be found by asking one question, and it is a question every organization new or old must ask at the onset of every fund-raising campaign. It needs to be asked about the organization in general and the specific purpose the campaign is supporting.

Remember the TV detective Kojak, played by the late Telly Savalas, who was always asking, "Who loves ya, baby?" Well, the question fund-raisers need to ask of their organizations is the same, although it is more likely to be phrased, *Who cares about us and why?*

Let's go back to the mission statement for a moment. If an organization's mission statement is truly in sync with what the organization is doing, it provides a way to help identify who cares about it and why. Or put another way, it explains who benefits from the existence of the organization.

For nearly all community organizations there are two primary beneficiary groups: (1) people who directly avail themselves of its services, and (2) a much larger grouping of people who, while they do not avail themselves of its services, nevertheless indirectly benefit because of what the organization does for the community. That latter group benefits because of its geographic proximity.

For example, an arts education organization obviously benefits those who enroll in its classes. They and their families would therefore be high on its list of donor prospects. However, all of those who live within the area from which it draws students also benefit because of the value such an organization has to the community. The availability of arts classes makes the community a better place to live and arguably has an effect on property values and the desirability of the community as a place to do business. Therefore, all of those persons living within the organization's service area are logically also prospective donors. Business and civic leaders likewise may never take a class, but they too benefit—even more strongly than the public at large it can be argued—because of the positive effect the organization has on a community in which they are even larger stakeholders than the average resident.

When it comes to the solicitation of corporate contributions, area of service and geography are often important deciding factors. A company rarely gives to a community organization that does not provide service to an area in which a substantial number of its employees either live or work. To put it bluntly, a corporation usually must have a facility or business-related connection in an area if it is to be successfully solicited.

It is possible for your organization to have a unique quality that would cause people with no stake in your geographic area to care about it enough to provide support. An inner-city housing initiative, for example, might draw the interest of national foundations and philanthropists from other communities because of its potential for replication. But you shouldn't count on distant benefactors. That would be the exception, and *you can't rely upon the exception for support.*

Money usually stays close to home, and conversely when it moves out of your area, don't expect it to come back for regular visits. Once a big donor, one who may have supported you for years, leaves town, his sense of philanthropic responsibility will be transferred to his new community. While he may remember you fondly and treasure his years of affiliation, he may no longer benefit from your services and therefore may no longer care about you in the same way.

How your organization raises and spends money is knowledge a successful fund-raiser must also have at his or her fingertips. You need to know and understand your organization's budget so that you can delineate the cost of operation and how the money to cover that cost is to be generated. Nearly all non-profits are, by their nature, limited in their capacity to increase earned revenues, and many are unable to produce any earned income because they serve groups that cannot afford to pay.

The inability to produce enough earned income to cover the cost of doing business is why non-profit organizations must be fund-raisers. However, understanding your organization's capacity to produce earned income, knowing where such income comes or could come from, and maximizing it are essential to developing a successful fund-raising campaign. If your prospective donors believe you could be producing more earned income, they will be far less likely to give of their limited philanthropic resources.

No matter what your role in a fund-raising campaign—be it organization director, development director, campaign chairperson, or solicitor—to operate at optimum effectiveness you need to be convinced your organization is maximizing its potential to produce earned income—*within the confines of its mission.* That last part is very important. There are things non-profit organizations simply cannot do which are second nature to businesses seeking to improve their bottom line.

At the Cleveland Orchestra, when we were subjected to questions regarding our profit-making capabilities, we responded half-jokingly that we could not increase our productivity, even if we played a Beethoven symphony faster than it was played 200 years ago. We could not speed up our assembly line, nor could we reduce the number of violinists required through automation. If the widget we produced was symphonic music, we could not cut costs by turning ourselves into a chamber orchestra and still produce our symphonic-music widget.

On the other hand, we did need to demonstrate constantly improving efficiency in other areas of our operations. For a non-profit, being perceived as a lean, mean fighting machine is critical to optimizing the results of a fund-raising campaign. But budget cuts must not come at the expense of maintaining and improving service to community and program quality. A non-profit that cuts back on the quality of its services will diminish its fund-raising appeal.

To summarize: If you are to raise money, you need to know your organization. There is no faster way to lose prospective donors than by being unable to answer questions and remove objections to giving. You need to know the organization's reason for being, its goals and objectives, its beneficiaries, and its operational and financial efficiencies. Know those things, and you know the organization. That knowledge will do more than prepare you to answer questions. It will give you the confidence and composure to pick up the telephone or knock on a door, and ultimately to sit in someone's office or living room and ask for money.

Knowing the organization is crucial to fund-raising, but without commitment, knowledge is worthless. There is a terribly hollow ring to words spoken in support of a cause in which the speaker does not believe. Volunteers occasionally find themselves pressed into service for an organization that their company or their boss supports but to which they have no real commitment. Keep in mind that, while these people can be effective fund-raisers, they do it by forcing themselves to "meet their quota." High on their list of priorities is figuring out a way to avoid the assignment next time. You will not be developing a pool of volunteers from which you can draw to staff future campaigns if your solicitors have been forced into service.

Knowledge and commitment are the two strongest tools a fund-raiser can have. Without knowledge, you cannot present your case to prospective donors. Without true commitment, you will not maximize the results of your efforts. If you are to raise money for an organization, know that organization and be committed to its cause.

CHAPTER 4

Planning for Fund-Raising and Achieving Consensus

A fund-raising campaign must be a plan, within a plan, within a plan. Each *campaign plan* works within the *general development plan*, which in turn must fit into the organization's *strategic plan*. Deviate from this hierarchy of plans and you invite chaos. A campaign plan that is not in accord with the general development plan may make its goal, but it may also "poison the well" for other fund-raising efforts. A general development plan that has not been created within the context of an organization's strategic plan may outline a valid theory for acquiring contributed income, but it will probably lack the content necessary for successful implementation.

A *strategic plan* is an organization's blueprint for carrying out its mission statement. It is initiated, implemented, and periodically reviewed by an organization's staff and board. The process of strategic planning, although it is out of the purview of this book, is a critically important element of successful management. Volumes have been written on the topic and any bookstore with a strong business and management section will have more than a few feet of shelf space devoted to the subject. I urge you to develop an understanding of the process and to make sure your organization has a strategic plan which it revisits annually.

A strategic plan, which should cover at least three years, is a prerequisite for establishing, first, a general fund-raising effort and, subsequently, specific fund-raising campaigns. It identifies institutional priorities, plots a course for achieving goals and objectives, lays out performance assessment, and provides for midcourse corrections. It is the first step in establishing an organization's budget. Knowing what is to be done and how it will be accomplished allows cost to be determined. Then, income can be balanced against expenses. The shortfall—the amount you plan to spend minus anticipated income—is the operational deficit. It represents the money the organization will have to raise, usually through contributed income, to balance its budget.

A *general development plan* identifies how and from what sources an organization will acquire and maximize contributed income. It encompasses all potential sources, identifies the tactics which will be used, and communicates that information to the organization's staff, volunteers, and influential supporters. Like the strategic plan, it is a living document subject to periodic review and updating. Usually, the person charged with the responsibility for managing the process of achieving contributed income will write the plan, in collaboration with the organization's director and the board development committee—if one has been established. If a standing development committee has not yet been named, the board as a whole or a temporary committee will have to exercise oversight responsibility.

The following general development plan is applicable to any organization, although each of the points would need to be adapted and augmented to fit a specific organization.

Typical General Development Plan

Strategy

1. Create a board of trustees able and willing to make major contributions and to solicit others for major contributions
2. Maximize the amounts contributed by donors
3. Create the largest possible effective base of corporate donors
4. Create the largest possible effective base of foundation donors
5. Create the largest possible effective base of individual donors
6. Create the largest possible effective base of volunteers

Tactics

1. Establish and maintain a development committee of the board of trustees
2. Institute programs to identify, rate, evaluate, and prioritize prospects, especially those who have the ability to make major contributions, both within the ranks of current support constituencies and from lists of prospective donors
3. Identify major prospects who may find it attractive to underwrite or sponsor a specific program, service, or department on an annual, ongoing, or one-time basis
4. Encourage trustees to maximize their donations
5. Encourage trustees to solicit prospects with whom they have influence and leverage
6. Assist trustees in developing a volunteer network of community leaders and executives who will solicit for the organization

7. Establish and maintain a development staff and/or train existing employees to help direct and staff all fund-raising initiatives
8. Develop compelling written materials that effectively communicate the organization's funding requirements to the board, other volunteers, and the public

Initiatives

1. Plan, initiate, and produce an endowment campaign and deferred-giving program to provide income in perpetuity to support programs and services
2. Plan, initiate, and produce other appropriate campaigns: i.e., annual, capital, underwriting, and sponsorship
3. Institute a communication program to maximize awareness of the organization's value to the community
4. Institute a recognition program to honor major donors

Well-thought-out plans are necessary for successful fund-raising, but the best-laid plans will come to naught if an organization's leaders have not arrived at a consensus to raise money. The paid head of the organization, the board chairperson, key staff members, trustees, volunteers, and advisory group members all need to agree with fund-raising goals and the plan for achieving those goals.

This is not the place to explore the techniques of consensus building. It is one of the hotter topics in the management community, and a trip to your local bookstore or library will turn up a plethora of books on the subject. Suffice it to say, consensus building is *involvement*. Consensus for any program of action is rarely achieved without involving in the program's design those from whom you are seeking the consensus.

Successful fund-raising relies heavily on trustee involvement. Trustees should be a fund-raising campaign's donors and solicitors of first resort. They must be an active part of the consensus-building process. Use your trustee development committee to develop overall fund-raising strategy, tactics, and initiatives and to plan specific campaigns.

Key staff members should also be involved in formulating general fund-raising strategy and tactics. If the people in charge of delivering the products and services of an organization are not in agreement with the process of soliciting contributed income, they will not be effective advocates for fund-raising efforts.

Then there are those, such as volunteer solicitors, who sign on for a fund-raising campaign. They play important roles, but by choice limit their involvement. A solicitor is not as fully engaged in a campaign as the campaign chair. It is unlikely that solicitors would take part in the formulation of campaign plans. However, you must win their consensus to carry out the campaign.

Two words describe what I have found to be the key to achieving consensus among volunteers, staff, and others involved in executing or supporting fund-raising efforts: *full disclosure.*

If you are the person putting a campaign together, inform everyone about its goals, how it will be carried out, and the roles, responsibilities, and relationships of all involved, and do it as early in the process as is possible. Never, ever think in terms of managing a person's need to know.

If you are a staff member, trustee, or volunteer, demand to know the fund-raising plan in its entirety from the beginning. Never, ever accept the answer, "That's something you won't be working on. You don't need to worry about it." If you are expending the time and effort to work on a fund-raising campaign, you want it to have every opportunity for success. An organization that doles out fund-raising information on a need-to-know basis is an organization that is crippling its own efforts. Frequent and detailed reports need to be issued to everyone involved in a fund-raising campaign.

CHAPTER 5

Funding Sources

No fund-raising campaign should ever be started until you have identified the *sources* from which you will draw contributions. Sources here does not refer to specific potential donors, but to the six categories of donors who contribute money to non-profit organizations. They are:

1. Trustees of the organization
2. Individuals
3. Corporations
4. Private foundations
5. Community foundations
6. Government

Your plan for a fund-raising campaign should target each source appropriate for that campaign and set a goal for contributions to be achieved from that source. Those goals are determined by rating and evaluating the potential donors that comprise each source, a process that will be more fully described in Chapter 6.

Trustees

All fund-raising campaigns begin with the trustees of an organization. In general, if you are planning a fund-raising campaign and are not expecting important contributions from your trustees, there is something drastically wrong with either your campaign plan or the composition of your board. Trustee giving sets the pace for any fund-raising campaign, and your board should have on it persons ready, willing, and able to make their best possible gifts to the organization.

A board of trustees is a resource for an organization to draw upon in carrying out its mission, and, remember, part of the mission of any successful non-profit organization is to raise money. Therefore, there must be people on an organization's board who can be counted on to give money. If your organization does not have trustees who can give, add them, even if it means enlarging the board.

Individuals

Individuals are the main source of philanthropic contributions in America. Most successful fund-raising campaigns receive from 70 to 80 percent of their money from individuals. They are the most flexible and spontaneous givers. Unlike corporations, foundations, and governmental entities, individuals are able to make a decision on the spot, and if they want, they can choose to put all their eggs in one basket. Joe Smith can reach for his checkbook a lot faster than the Metropolis Community Foundation with its rigid timetables and layers of committee meetings, and Mr. Smith has no requirement to spread his charitable contributions among a variety of worthwhile causes.

Corporations

Corporations look at requests for support from three points of view: Is it good philanthropy? Does it enhance the corporate image? Will it generate revenue for the corporation? A contribution made for straight philanthropic reasons is a gift of good citizenship from which a corporation expects little or no direct benefit. A contribution made with image as a major consideration is made with the expectation that it will engender positive feelings on the part of the public toward the corporation. A contribution made based upon its potential to generate revenue is as much business deal as charitable gift.

Straight philanthropic giving is the kind non-profits usually receive from corporations for annual fund campaigns and operational support. It is the main type of giving, which corporations use to satisfy their commitments and responsibilities to support community initiatives that enhance the well-being of constituencies important to them—employees, shareholders, and customers. Usually, an organization will receive many contributions made for this purpose, and no single corporation expects greater publicity and recognition than that directly attributable to the value of its gift. Corporations rarely ever make this kind of donation in communities where they have little or no presence.

Giving to build image is high-visibility giving, and a corporation expects to receive wide public recognition for such a gift. Often the contribution will take the form of sponsoring an event or program in expectation that the corporation will have its name attached to it. Corporations that have a relationship with a large segment of the public as a result of the products or services they offer are particularly responsive to image-related contribution requests. The greater the visibility a non-profit can promise for an image-related contribution, the greater the likelihood of a positive and substantial response to solicitation. Great care should be taken by the non-profit organization not to promise too much. Out-of-pocket expenses brought on by promoting the sponsored event or program—everything from billboards to tote bags—can severely diminish the proceeds from the sponsorship.

Giving which produces revenue is bottom-line giving for corporations. For most non-profit organizations, this kind of support should rank a distant third. Essentially, the non-profit organization sells, advertises, or endorses a company's products or services and receives contributions out of the business revenues thereby generated. Unfortunately, the proceeds are seldom in line with the effort expended, and you run the risk of alienating similar companies to the point where you cannot go to them for contributions of any kind. In addition, contracts for this type of program are usually written by the corporation so that it can withdraw its participation on short notice, leaving the non-profit organization high and dry.

Private Foundations

Private foundations are for the most part repositories of funds from a single source or at most a very few—for example, an individual or family. They often operate with greater freedom than community foundations and act quite quickly. While many have formal guidelines, some will make grants on the strength of a relatively informal request. Private foundations give to all types of organizations, programs, and fund-raising campaigns. Often they are good sources of start-up funds and seed money. Some give to specific subjects and causes, while others limit their grant-making geographically.

Community Foundations

Community foundations are repositories of funds contributed by individuals and corporations for use primarily to improve the quality of life within their community. They can cover a single city, a region, a state, or even an entire country. Most commonly, they make grants to non-profit organizations from the income earned on endowment. Sometimes they make a distribution of principal from endowment or invest endowment funds in a community initiative.

The funds at a community foundation's disposal can often be restricted, meaning that grants have to be made within an interest area, such as arts, or to a specific organization, such as a community's art museum. Unrestricted funds are distributed according to the foundation's best determination of need.

It takes time for a community foundation to analyze a grant application. A number of individuals and committees usually review a proposal—which must be submitted following specific guidelines—before it is accepted or rejected. Grants are made on a regular schedule, usually quarterly, and you can expect months to pass between first contact and grant approval.

Government

Governments at the local, state, and federal level contribute funds to non-profits. Federal agencies such as the National Endowment for the Humanities and the National Institutes of Health make grants in their particular areas of interest. The states have similar area-of-interest grant-making agencies. Sometimes an organization, such as a state arts council, isn't actually part of state government, but exists as a semi-independent authority to administer the distribution of state and federal funds. On the local level, agencies ranging from park boards to the mayor's office may have a process for making contributions to non-profits. In general, the lower the level of government, the faster the turnaround time for a grant proposal. As is the case with foundations, governmental grant-making agencies usually require that an organization follow a set of predetermined guidelines when requesting funds.

Elected officials are the ultimate controllers of the funds governments make available for grant-making, so lobbying legislators, as well as informing and involving other key government officials, is an important tactic for any organization that sees government as a funding source. Trustees who have clout with elected or appointed officials can be invaluable in presenting an organization's need for funding.

Your analysis of the best possible fund-raising sources is dependent on the cause for which you are seeking money, and the ways in which you are going after it. In some campaigns, all six source groups may be fair game. In others, it is conceivable that only one or two will be targeted. A long, hard look at your organization and its mission, your community and its philanthropic traditions, and the number of foundations, corporations, and governmental entities with a history of supporting your organization or the type of programs it offers will help you assess your chances with each category of funding sources.

One of the most famous lines ever delivered in America was Willy Sutton's response when asked why he robbed banks. "That's where the money is," he said. Obviously, grocery stores, gas stations, doctor's offices, post offices, and federal mints also are repositories of cash. What the infamous bank robber was really saying was, "Banks have the most money likely to be easily accessed by me with the tools I have at hand."

Every fund-raising campaign requires you to examine your tools—the cause you are touting, the arguments you have marshaled in support of it, and the people and means available to present those arguments—and then determine which sources are likely to have the most money you can access.

I remember when the American Symphony Orchestra League (ASOL) asked its more than 1,500 members what topics they wanted to see addressed at the League's annual regional workshops. More than 80 percent listed fund-raising. When asked what specific fund-raising topic they wanted to focus on, 80 percent said corporate giving. Yet many of ASOL's orchestras, ensembles, and bands are in small communities where there is little or no corporate presence.

Why did they choose corporate fund-raising? Because most of us find it easier to ask a corporation for money than a private individual, and because as a society we have come to view corporations as the holders of vast wealth. When a corporate contributions officer says no, it seems less personal. However, a fund-raising campaign strategy should not be based on anticipating the least painful turndown. Nor should fund-raising strategy be based on an erroneous understanding of wealth. It is the owners of a corporation, *individuals* who hold a corporation's stock, who have the money to give to worthy causes.

Willy Sutton was right. You go where money you think you can get is to be found in the greatest quantities, and most of the time that means you look to the individual donor.

CHAPTER 6

Prospecting for Donors: There's Gold in Them Thar Hills

Whether they are stewards of others' money or individual contributors, people who are willing to give to an organization almost invariably fall into one of two groups: those who are personally touched, inspired, and motivated by the organization's programs and services; and those who, while not personally touched by the organization, are influenced and impressed by what it does. If you are going to be a successful fund-raiser, you need to know who cares about your organization and who shares your belief that it benefits the community.

Individual donors can fit easily into either of those categories. Foundations, corporations, and government funders fall almost exclusively into the second group, although it is possible that the people either recommending or approving grants and contributions may have been personally touched by an organization asking for funding.

Those who directly benefit from an organization are most often users of its programs and services, or their family members are users. The majority of people who have been users of an organization begin with the belief that the fees they pay or that are paid on their behalf are the primary, if not entire, support of the organization. More often than not, that is far from the truth. Users of an organization who gain an understanding of how small a percentage of the total costs their fees cover and who have the economic wherewithal to do so can become an organization's most responsive donors. Hospitals always put former patients high on their list of potential donors. Schools and universities have entire departments devoted to alumni relations.

At the Cleveland Orchestra, we collected the names and addresses of everyone we could who purchased tickets each year. Even though these folks were paying as much as $50 for a seat at Severance Hall, many of them became significant donors, contributing as a group as much as 40 percent of a campaign goal. They realized that ticket prices could be two or three times higher if it weren't for the generosity of donors such as themselves.

Every organization should have a database of users to prospect for donors. Even if the organization serves a clientele unlikely to be able to make gifts, those client-users may lead to previously untapped sources of funding. For example, they might be residents of a municipality or neighborhood that is a focus of funding for a community foundation. Or they might be employees or relatives of employees of a corporation that has a charitable giving program.

One of the first organizations I ever worked with was Big Brothers of Greater Cleveland. At the time it served more than 500 boys who did not have fathers at home. Although the boys' mothers weren't financially able to give much money to Big Brothers, we did a little research and discovered that more than 10 percent of the women were employees of a local utility company. Our funding request to the utility pointed out this fact and included endorsements from many of those employees. The result was a gift that, compared to the company's other contributions, was disproportionately large.

Organizations need to be able to analyze their database of users for such links to potential donors. If the information is available, the database should include names and addresses of users, their place of employment, and the place of employment of members of their immediate family.

Non-profit organizations should also assemble a database of persons acting as stewards of other people's money at foundations, corporations, and governmental agencies that give to non-profits in their community. Professional program officers of foundations and governmental funders (this includes directors and other senior paid management involved in recommending and approving grants); trustees of foundations; and corporate contributions managers, CEOs, and other highly placed managers all need to be made aware of an organization's value.

Some of the tactics you could employ when courting stewards of other people's money include:

1. Invite them to visit your facility
2. Introduce them to people who have benefited from your organization
3. Provide comp tickets to performances and invite them to meet performers
4. Invite them to come see your organization at work
5. Invite them to your annual meeting
6. Schedule a lunch for them with members of your board of trustees
7. Make sure they are on your mailing list
8. Invite them to a golf outing or other "social" event with your trustees and staff

Obviously, not all these suggestions apply to every organization.

Not long ago a client of mine learned a valuable lesson. I encouraged the executive director of an organization with which I was consulting to call a number of corporate contributions managers and invite them to come to lunch at his facility. The executive director later told me he had made the invitations with no expectation they would be accepted. Surprised by how many agreed to come, he remarked to some of them, "But you must get invitations like this all the time." They assured him otherwise.

The executive director had assumed it would be almost impossible to get these people to take two or three hours of their time and come out to his operation. Instead, he learned that many contributions managers felt they weren't asked to visit often enough; they wanted to learn more about organizations they funded. Many of my corporate contributions manager friends tell me they are continually trying to gain greater knowledge of non-profit organizations. They say that their grants committees are always turning to them for more information.

There are important differences between individual donors and foundations and corporations that affect the fund-raising process. To begin with, the individual can make an immediate decision. That doesn't hold true for corporate contributions managers and foundation program officers whom fund-raisers have to rely on to present their organization's case to one or more committees. Only then will a decision be rendered, and usually the ultimate decision makers are insulated from the grant seekers. (Exceptions to this would be small foundations or corporations that operate without an intervening layer of professional contributions managers or grant officers.)

You have to take care to determine just how zealously contributions managers and program officers guard access to their superiors. Ask them what level of contact they are comfortable with and how they would like you to handle any inadvertent contact. My rule of thumb is never, never, leapfrog over anybody. In general, woe befalls the fund-raiser who goes around the program officers, contributions managers, or a corporation's local management.

When grant seekers write to the chairperson at one foundation I know, they get a letter back from the program officer beginning, "Our foundation president has forwarded your request for funds to me because, as you should know, it is my responsibility to review all proposals prior to the trustees considering them." Being chastised for not following the rules isn't exactly the best way to begin a dialogue with a person whose recommendation is crucially important to your funding request.

Even if you strictly adhere to a policy of following only authorized paths in search of support, you can still stumble across the occasional land mine. When that happens, defuse it before it blows up in your face. More than once I have found myself in a pickle because members of my board who were corporate CEOs planned on instructing their contributions managers to donate to a campaign. My job was to get on the phone, let the contributions managers know what was coming, explain that it was neither my doing nor something I could control, and apologize anyway! Then there were the times when a member of my board would tell me that on the golf course the next day he planned to speak to Mr. X, CEO of the ABC corporation, about making a gift. Again, I would be on the phone, to Mr. X's contributions manager. Once, the person chairing a campaign for my client organization was also a trustee of a local foundation. As a result, the foundation's trustees began talking about our campaign and the fact that we were going to be asking for support before we had submitted a proposal to the program officer. I could go on and on with examples of how easy it is to inadvertently step over the line.

Program officers and contributions managers are well aware that situations such as these occur, and that they are beyond a fund-raiser's control. They also are aware that fund-raisers occasionally encourage these situations and then claim innocence. What they don't want is to be blindsided. Nor do they want to see a pattern of "Oops, sorry, nothing I could do about it" situations.

In addition to the degree of contact they will allow, there is another important difference between contributions managers and program officers on the one hand and major individual donors on the other: the pleasure they derive from the giving experience itself. Individuals derive a personal reward from the process of giving that isn't the same for those who hold stewardship over other people's money. Individual donors are enriched by the process of giving and by the relationship they develop with the organizations to which they give. Their giving experience is personal; they often develop a sense of "ownership" toward the organizations they support.

For this reason, individual donors need to be provided with information that will allow them to come to an understanding of the value of an organization and its programs. The case for support should be presented in a way that appeals to the individual's desire for enrichment. It must be logical, but have an emotional appeal. To make an effective case, a fund-raiser should develop an understanding of an individual donor's needs and desires and how they could be fulfilled by giving to the organization.

In other words, do your homework. Find out everything you can about a major individual donor's interests, past philanthropic activities, and philosophy of life. The essence of a good solicitation is knowing as much as possible about the individual or family from whom you will be requesting a contribution. Fund-raisers should be able to answer the following questions about every prospective donor they plan to contact:

1. In what aspect(s) of the organization is the prospect known to be interested?
2. How strong is that interest, and how has it been demonstrated?
3. Has the prospect established a relationship with someone in the organization? Who?
4. Does the prospect have a business or social relationship with one or more of the organization's major contributors? Who?
5. What are the prospect's personal interests and avocations?

6. Does the prospect have control or influence over philanthropic funds? Which ones?

7. Has the prospect taken any public stands on issues of concern to the organization? What are they?

8. What other organizations has the prospect supported and for how much?

Fund-raisers need to be able to see their organization and the world from the prospect's point of view. They must anticipate how a prospect is likely to react to a request that he support a particular cause, program, or project.

Program officers and contributions managers, while they may believe in an organization, are not being asked to invest their *own* money in it. The fund-raiser is, in the end, simply apprising them of the reasons for supporting the organization. The job is to place before them a logical case for support that convinces them to recommend a donation. Stewards of other people's money need to justify the gifts they recommend on rational grounds. Here, any emotional appeal is likely to be secondary.

So what motivates individuals, foundations, corporations, and governmental funders to give? Let me count the whys:

1. ***Philanthropic nature:*** Giving fulfills a human need to be of service.
2. ***Good citizenship:*** Involved and caring residents of a community are committed to improving its quality of life. I couldn't even begin to count the times donors to the Cleveland Orchestra said, "We really don't go to concerts very often, but the Orchestra is good for Cleveland."
3. ***Mandated contributions:*** Each year, corporations and often governmental funders have budgeted a certain amount for contributions. Foundations and sometimes governmental funders are required by law to make donations.
4. ***Employee recruitment:*** Corporations, law firms, hospitals, universities, and just about every other type of employer find that non-profit organizations are important draws when recruiting employees. Many times corporate executives told me that the Cleveland Orchestra was the "little extra" that pushed a sought-after recruit in the direction of Cleveland and their firm.
5. ***Example of others:*** The philanthropic spirit seems to be infectious. If everybody around you is giving, it is hard not to make a contribution yourself.

Once an organization has determined who will give and why they will give, the next question to answer is when will they give. We know prospective donors aren't likely to give unless they're asked. No matter how strong their philanthropic nature or how solid their citizenship, people still have to be asked to contribute. The same holds true of corporations, foundations, and governmental funders. Money does not walk up and bite you—even when you are a valued and respected non-profit organization. *You* have to make the approach.

However, not just anyone should ask just any donor. Ideally, prospective donors should be asked to give by someone likely to have a high degree of influence over them. The key here is to choose a solicitor whom the prospect respects. Qualities to look for include:

1. *Past association with the prospect:* The solicitor could be someone a prospect knows professionally, shares the same neighborhood with, or has in some other way met.
2. *Charisma:* People who have a compelling presence and an infectious personality can influence both the willingness to give and the size of the gift.
3. *Stature:* People are flattered when someone they consider important asks them for a contribution.
4. *Commitment:* The higher the degree of devotion and dedication to an organization and its programs that a solicitor manifests, the more successful he or she will be in convincing others.

Respected and influential solicitors must do more than simply ask for donations; they must present a compelling case for support. And that is the final part of the answer to the question of when people will give: when they are convinced of the benefit and value of an organization and its programs.

To summarize, prospective donors will give when they have been convinced of the value of and need for their gift, when they are personally asked, and when the solicitation comes from the "right" person—someone they respect and who can make a strong, credible case for support.

Finally, a word about the gifts you may get. A fund-raising campaign usually sets its sights on a certain type of gift—most commonly cash—but donors at times prefer to give whatever commodity works to their best advantage. An organization should almost never refuse a gift, even if it isn't what was asked for. Most things can be turned into cash, although not necessarily the day after you get them, and certainly not if they have been given with a caveat on rushing them to market. For instance, an organization might be given stock in a closely held company with the understanding that it would not sell the stock until a specified event has occurred. Any gift an organization receives for which there is a ready market can be turned into cash relatively quickly. However, there are good times and bad times to sell. Down markets occur for every commodity, from art to real estate.

The toughest decisions come over non-liquid assets, the maintenance and management of which may require considerable expense on the part of the recipient. Examples include equipment an organization can neither use itself nor easily sell, real estate for which there is little or no market, artwork which the organization doesn't want to display and insure but is forbidden to sell, damaged or outdated goods a merchant wishes to unload, and absolutely anything for which the market is questionable at best. This is where a polite, "Thanks for thinking of us, but we aren't the right place for that very generous gift. We would never be able to get full value or use out of it," may be the right response. However, if you ask for $5,000, and someone gives you stock, or a paid-up insurance policy, or salable land in the next county, take it.

No matter what you are offered, never show disappointment. This is particularly true when you are given a pledge in response to a request for a cash contribution. Your organization may need cash now, but it is also going to need cash later. A pledge is a commitment to give at a future time. Think of it as a receivable, almost money in the bank. Donors have reasons for pledging a contribution rather than reaching for their checkbooks. Don't insult them by telling them those reasons aren't good enough. Take the pledge, go out and raise the money you need today from someone else, and collect the pledge when it comes due.

What should you do when you don't get as much as you were expecting from a donor? Never, but never, display any body language or voice inflection that would let a donor know that you are unhappy with a gift's size. And definitely don't respond by saying, "Thanks, but we were really counting on what you gave to the campaign last year." Stating that sentiment can hurt donors who have undergone financial reverses and are being forced to reduce their contributions budget, and it will surely hurt your organization. Donors have long memories. Going back to them with a future request for funding after they have been wounded by someone in your organization can be difficult. If there is one thing you don't want to do, it is damage a relationship by being shortsighted.

Some years ago I had been slowly but steadily developing a relationship with a donor to the Cleveland Orchestra. This generous and thoughtful person liked projects. For a number of years, she had been reviewing our annual "shopping list" of needs from which she would choose something in the $20,000 range to "buy." One year, the project she liked cost $40,000. After reviewing our request for that amount, she dutifully gave her usual $20,000.

This time that was not enough for me. So in my thank-you letter, I suggested that she give us an additional $20,000 to cover the rest of the cost, promising we would then not solicit her the following year. The note I received back made it clear my strategy had not pleased her. She declined my request for the additional money and intimated that the $20,000 might not now be forthcoming.

My life flashed before me! When I regained my senses, I composed an abject note of apology, which, accompanied by a florist's best efforts, was on the way before lunch.

A few days later she wrote back, "All is forgiven. The flowers are beautiful, and here is my check for $20,000. As far as next year, we'll have to wait until then."

The valuable lesson learned the hard way (for a while I thought it would be the heart-attack way) is never forget that the donor's wishes and interests come first.

CHAPTER 7

Rating and Evaluating Prospects: Whom Do You Ask for How Much

No one would argue the fact that every fund-raising campaign needs a goal and that everyone connected with the campaign, including prospective donors, needs to be aware of that goal. Then why do people so often fight the setting of a goal for each prospective donor and sharing that goal with the prospect? Trustees often blanch at the idea, and it is the rare solicitor who the first time he or she is told that there will be a suggested giving amount for each of his prospects does not respond with, "I can't *tell* people what to give!"

They're right. Solicitors shouldn't try to *tell* prospects what to give, as this will engender a great deal of resistance. Yet setting a personal goal for all prospective individual donors, letting prospects know what *their* goal is, and helping them see where and how it fits under the umbrella of the campaign goal is probably the most important element of a campaign. No matter what sources you are approaching, you need to be ready with a suggested giving amount in line with what each prospective donor is capable of giving. Dealing with foundations, corporations, and government funders in this manner is easy. In fact, it is usually required. Grant application forms have a blank space where you fill in the amount requested. But when it comes to individual donors, we seem to think it is a different kettle of fish. It isn't.

Individual Donor

If a fund-raising campaign is to have a realistic chance at succeeding, we *must* in the case of every prospective individual donor:

1. Rate and evaluate the ability to give
2. Seek a realistically large—hopefully the maximum—potential gift
3. Provide the donor with a suggested gift amount

Prospect rating meetings for individual donors are usually the most important meetings that will be held for any fund-raising campaign. They work best when participation is limited to a few people comfortable with discussing the personal finances of others. Such meetings are fraught with the opportunity for unnecessary comments. That temptation should be resisted. Remember, those doing the evaluating in one meeting are likely themselves to be rated in some future campaign. Courtesy, discretion, and respect are the watchwords here.

Perhaps the most damaging and the most common negative aspect of these meetings occurs when participants after rating a prospect at a certain level expound on why you won't get a gift at that level. You'll hear everything from, "They're giving a million dollars this year to the XYZ institution," to "He's the cheapest guy in town." The proper response is, "If they have the potential to give that amount, never mind the reasons why they won't. We must never say no for prospects. That's their job. It's ours to talk them out of it—to give them the opportunity."

You begin rating prospects by establishing a sizable database of caring and financially capable individuals. This list will be generated from an organization's past fund-raising experience, suggestions of new prospects from participants in rating meetings, and analysis of those known to give to similar organizations and causes.

Years ago, when we were planning to go to Akron, Ohio, for the first time to raise money for the Cleveland Orchestra's summer home, Blossom Music Center, which is actually located considerably closer to downtown Akron than to Cleveland—we had a problem identifying prospects. We had been selling tickets in Akron for only two years, and the Orchestra had virtually no donor constituency there. We took the annual reports of the seven or eight largest cultural institutions in Akron and went through each, identifying donors and the sizes of their gifts. This was long before the advent of the desktop computer, so we made a three-by-five card for each donor listed by each institution. Then we assembled the cards in alphabetical order. Many names appeared on seven or eight cards, with most of them indicating they were giving $1,000 a year to each institution. You can bet we rated each one of these donors at $1,000 when it came to making our prospect list.

Once you have made the determination that an individual is capable of giving at a certain level and has the proclivity to give to your organization or similar programs, you must be willing to go after that amount. This is what is meant by seeking a realistically large—hopefully the maximum—potential gift. Is it really the maximum? Probably not. You would have to be an awfully good evaluator and a particularly brave fund-raiser to go after a truly maximum potential gift every time. But you must seek the largest potential gift you feel is achievable from each donor. To do otherwise *needlessly* inflates the list of prospective donors required, increases the amount of work to be done, and lengthens the amount of time a campaign will take.

Now back to the problem of telling people what to give. Remember, *you aren't telling, you're suggesting!* No one wants to be told what to give to any fund-raising campaign, but most prospects will welcome a suggestion of what would be appropriate. People nearly always want to know what the "price" of something is. It is rare that anyone decides to purchase an item without first looking at the price tag. The same is true when it comes to making a philanthropic donation. People want to know how much the soliciting organization needs, and fund-raisers should always have a ready answer.

That answer should be a specific dollar amount determined by a rating and evaluating process, but far too often it is:

1. *Give what you can:* Requesting that multimillionaires give what they can is silly. You seldom are likely to be asking any one person for resources of that magnitude.
2. *Give what you are comfortable with:* People can be comfortable with giving $10 when you need $100 and they could give that and more.
3. *We would appreciate a gift in the range of _____ to_____:* Asking for a gift in the range of $100 to $1,000 tells the prospect you haven't determined what your real needs are.

You should always suggest a specific number, and that suggestion must be presented in a way that is neither annoying nor demanding. There is only one person who can and will decide the size of a gift—the individual making that gift. However, most prospects will welcome and consider a request made in the following manner:

> **We are going to the community to raise $250,000 that we plan to place in a permanent endowment fund to provide income in perpetuity, assuring that we will continue to meet our financial needs; be able to maintain, improve, and enhance our current programs and services; and have the opportunity to implement new ones to meet the growing needs of our community.**
>
> **To help us meet our campaign goal, we hope that you will consider making a gift of $10,000.**
>
> **We are suggesting this amount because, as you can appreciate, a campaign of this magnitude and limited time frame requires a certain number of leadership gifts at significant dollar levels. While this suggested amount was developed with that premise in mind, we recognize and understand that in the final analysis you will consider what is right for you. Of course, whatever you can give will be deeply appreciated.**

I have used this suggested gift statement, with obvious modification, in numerous campaigns, and it has worked well. It succeeds because it approaches prospects as each of us would want to be approached—thoughtfully, courteously, and enthusiastically.

Remember, chances are that a careful and thoughtful ratings process will result in your asking for an amount heard many times before by the prospect. Your request is not going to be shocking or offensive. Even if it is high, when presented respectfully and politely, you are likely to be told, "Gee, if I really had that kind of money, I would be glad to give it to you." At that point the prospect has said he will give. Now all remains is for him to decide how much, and you have started his thinking at a far higher level than a low-ball request would have prompted.

Foundations and Corporations

When it comes to rating and evaluating prospects, fund-raisers spend the lion's share of their time on individual donors. After all, in nearly every campaign, they are the primary source of contributions. However, it behooves us to take a look at the process as it pertains to other giving sources. For our purposes, let's assume that governmental funders can be handled like foundations and private and community foundations can be viewed as essentially the same.

For foundations, the best and most comprehensive source of information is The Foundation Center. It maintains reference libraries in New York City, Washington, D.C., San Francisco, and Cleveland. The Center also publishes *The Foundation Directory*, a reference book listing each foundation in the United States and including:

1. Its name, address, officers, and trustees
2. Its purpose and year of incorporation
3. Its total assets
4. The number of grants it typically makes, total annual distributions, and the size of its largest and smallest grants in a given year
5. What programs and activities it supports (i.e., endowment, capital projects, operating expenses, annual campaigns, new programs, personnel expense)
6. Information which must accompany a grant application
7. Specific projects, programs, and entities to which it will not make grants
8. Proposal submission and review dates

My experience with The Foundation Center library and its staff in Cleveland has been nothing but positive and most beneficial. The library maintains a complete microfilm record of all IRS Form 990s. (This is the tax form that all private foundations must file, showing to whom each gave money in any given year.) I have frequently used the library's 990 microfilm to search for donor prospects among private foundations.

The best sources of information about corporations are the local chambers of commerce and a book called *The Corporate Giving Directory*, published by the Taft Group in Rockville, Maryland. The *Directory* lists which corporations gave what to whom in each state. Be mindful, however, that when it comes to gaining corporate support in your community, there is no substitute for the same kind of hands-on knowledge which you should be collecting about prospective individual donors. The best sources for this type of corporate information are remarkably similar to those you would seek out for data about individual donors. In addition, the chamber of commerce can provide a list of its members, usually the businesses of any size in a community. This and any other available list should be reviewed for the names of new potential donors by a committee which has an understanding of the local corporate community and its giving patterns. Once again, don't overlook past experience and the experiences of similar organizations.

As part of the process of rating and evaluating prospective donors, you should take into consideration the causes they are known to support or avoid. Except in the case of individual donors, the record is pretty clear. Many foundations and corporations have published guidelines which indicate whether they will give to the following types of campaigns and requests:

1. Annual
2. Capital
3. Challenge
4. Endowment
5. In-kind
6. Multiyear grants
7. Sponsorship and underwriting

These guidelines also spell out where grants are restricted as to location, type of organization, or content of program.

With individual donors, the lines are usually less clearly drawn. Even if an individual has refused to give to a category of request in the past, he or she still might be worth a try, particularly if the circumstances are unusual. People do change their minds. However, it is generally wise not to solicit individuals who have made it clear they will not give either to the type of campaign being conducted or its underlying purpose.

CHAPTER 8

Annual Campaigns:
Once a Year Every Year

An annual campaign is best described as a campaign conducted each and every year for the purpose of raising money to assist in paying a non-profit organization's regular, ongoing expenses. The money it raises is most commonly used to offset an operational deficit, but it can be applied to any purpose. The annual campaign is usually an organization's primary source of unrestricted contributed income and should be a mainstay of its fund-raising efforts.

The goals of any annual campaign ought to include:

1. Stimulating the contribution of unrestricted funds
2. Raising an awareness and acceptance of the institution and its responsibility to raise money
3. Developing a base of knowledgeable volunteers
4. Cultivating prospects for future giving

Every non-profit organization with a need to raise contributed income should have an annual campaign which it conducts *every* year.

Use the chart on page 40 to help estimate an obtainable goal. For each source of annual fund income, list the previous year's achievement, identify what portion of that income will not be repeatable, and estimate expected new gifts and increases. From this information you should be able to project the total amount of contributions that can be realistically achieved.

Executing a well-conceived annual campaign allows an organization to build a predictable base of support and provides a pool of proven donors for other fund-raising efforts. The vast majority of individual donors give their first contribution to an organization through its annual campaign. Repeat contributors to annual campaigns become an identified group of loyal and established givers—a constituency. Their record

CURRENT FISCAL YEAR

ANNUAL FUND CAMPAIGN EVALUATION AND GOAL

Division	Prior Year's Result	Major Losses	Net Available	Estimated Increases	Net Plus Increases
Corporations	$ 15,760	$ 1,200	$ 14,560	$ 3,000	$ 17,560
Foundations	4,110	500	3,610	500	4,110
Trustees	7,911	2,000	5,911	1,000	6,911
Individuals	25,419	1,800	23,619	5,000	28,619
Special Event	5,200	5,200	N/A	N/A	N/A
Raffle (new)	N/A	N/A	N/A	3,000	3,000
Miscellaneous	1,280	N/A	1,280	300	1,580
Final Result	**$ 59,680**	**$ 10,700**	**$ 48,980**	**$12,800**	**$ 61,780 (Forecast)**

of contribution shows a care and concern for the organization that makes them prime prospects for capital and endowment campaigns.

No matter what other fund-raising efforts are being planned for a given year, the annual campaign must go on. I have often had to convince people that an annual campaign can be successfully run in tandem with a campaign for a special purpose, such as endowment or capital. Their rationale for wanting to abandon the annual campaign is that the organization does not have the resources to conduct simultaneous campaigns. They also believe that supporters will not give to more than one fund-raising effort in the same year.

If an organization truly does not have the resources to conduct both an annual and a special-purpose campaign within the same 12-month period, it should not cancel the annual campaign. Rather, the fund-raising resources—for the most part, the base of volunteers—should be enlarged so that both campaigns can be conducted. In fact, the need to run two campaigns can be the impetus for making a much-needed expansion in an organization's base of volunteers. In my 20 years with the Cleveland Orchestra, we ran endowment or capital campaigns a number of times, without ever shutting down the annual campaign, and the collective amount given to the annual campaign by those who also contributed to an endowment or capital campaign always increased.

An annual campaign is a broad-based fund-raising effort directed at a large number of prospective donors. Both the overall goal and the average gift are usually far smaller than those in an endowment or capital campaign. Similarly, an annual campaign should be considerably shorter in duration than either capital or endowment efforts. The usual length is from several weeks to several months, but be prepared for the fact that annual campaigns almost always take longer than planned. An annual campaign relies upon a great many solicitors, and those solicitors will not all operate at optimum efficiency. They have other commitments, and the people they are trying to reach are not always available on the first try. Realistically, from the time solicitors start contacting prospects to close of effort, I like to see an annual campaign last no more than six weeks.

Because of its broad-based nature, an annual campaign cannot rely upon individually rating prospects as strongly as do capital and endowment campaigns. Annual campaigns can have hundreds, thousands, even tens of thousands of potential donors. You rate and evaluate as many of those prospects as you can. At the Cleveland Orchestra, volunteer groups, such as our Women's Committee, were asked to go over the list of subscribers who were non-donors. Those subscribers whom someone could recommend as being able to contribute a specific amount were solicited for that amount. Subscribers for whom we had no information other than where they lived or the cost of their seats in Severance Hall would be put down for an arbitrary, but we hoped realistic, suggested giving level.

Failing to suggest a specific gift size is the most common mistake made in annual campaigns. I know of organizations that have sent letters to former donors asking them to ". . . renew your gift at last year's level," without even telling the donors what they gave last year. How will those donors know what to do? The one thing they can surmise from such a request is that the organization must have raised plenty of money last year since it isn't asking for more this year. *Always ask for more each year.* Your expenses are going up; you need to raise more money. Failing to target an amount—an increased amount—is the single most devastating mistake made in an annual campaign.

To increase a donor's contribution to an annual campaign, one of the most useful tools is the creation of a membership program. Donors giving at a certain level to the annual fund receive the appellation of Friend of (organization name). The title can be inflated at specified giving levels by having categories of friends such as Contributing Friend, Supporting Friend, and Sustaining Friend. For very large gifts you can create distinct categories such as Benefactors League, Founders Society, and President's Circle. The idea here is to appropriately recognize donors for their generosity. You should always print their names under the appropriate membership category in your annual report and other media. Perhaps you even place the names of those in the highest categories on a wall in your building. This much-appreciated public thank-you exerts a little subtle peer group pressure on donors to give at a level that meets their capability, and attracts and compels others to want their names listed as well.

Depending on the type of organization, it is even possible to offer "benefits" of membership, which increase at each level. Performing arts and other cultural organizations have obvious benefits they can offer, such as tickets to performances and events, but it may require some creative thinking on the part of social service organizations to come up with perks. One way might be to have a corporation sponsor your membership program and provide benefits. However, remember that membership benefits should not be the primary reason someone gives to your annual fund. If they are, then your membership program is actually a marketing program through which you are selling something for the money you receive.

Membership programs that sell are appropriate for some organizations: for instance, museums which charge admission, but waive that charge for members. However, to my way of thinking, such membership fees are really earned income, and as such should be the province of an organization's marketing department. People who join these kinds of membership programs have more in common with season ticket holders of a performing arts organization than with donors to that performing arts organization's annual campaign. Such members would, of course, be fine prospective donors for the annual campaign.

There are two good reasons for establishing a non-marketing membership program. Having memberships at different giving levels provides an organization with a status to associate with a suggested donation to the annual fund, and this is sometimes persuasive to prospects. However, the greatest value is that they bolster the solicitor. Memberships are a sales tool that the volunteer solicitor can use for support when making a presentation to a prospect. They help the solicitor feel good about asking at a suggested level, and that means an organization is more likely to achieve its goal for the annual campaign.

The goal—the money that needs to be raised—is always the primary reason for an annual campaign. However, there are secondary positive results. An annual campaign raises the public profile of an organization. It offers a number of opportunities to issue press releases with a real news hook—goal announcement, campaign kickoff, steps in reaching goal, entering the homestretch, goal reached, volunteers and donors thanked. Annual campaigns give an organization an ongoing way to "exercise" its fund-raising muscles. If there is a strong base of volunteer fund-raisers in place, then capital or endowment campaigns have a foundation upon which to build.

CHAPTER 9

Endowment Campaigns: Building for the Future

An endowment campaign is a fund-raising campaign that raises money for an organization to invest rather than spend. The proceeds from an endowment campaign are placed in an endowment fund, the income from which is used by the organization to meet ongoing expenses, cover capital expenditures, or fund special projects and programs.

An organization which undertakes an endowment campaign does so in order to lessen its need either to raise money each year to cover any operational deficit—the difference between earned income and expenses—or to raise money for occasional extraordinary expenses. Income earned on money placed in an endowment fund is restricted to the purpose or purposes of that fund, and the fund is not easily invaded. Usually, an organization's bylaws make it hard, if not impossible, for the organization to spend endowment.

Because of the special nature of endowment funds, an organization should undertake an endowment campaign only when:

1. The organization is old enough to have exhibited sufficient financial stability for donors to feel comfortable giving to endowment which will yield income in perpetuity. Endowment is for eternity, and before beginning an endowment campaign, an organization needs to be well-enough established to anticipate a long life; an organization with a history is more likely to look like an organization with a future.

2. The organization anticipates and expects that in the short term it can cover any operational deficit through an annual campaign and other gifts and grants. It simply is not good business to expend limited resources on an endowment campaign when those resources may be desperately needed to raise money to offset an operational deficit. Another argument for having a strong annual

campaign in place before attempting to raise money for endowment is that a successful annual campaign program aids endowment fund-raising efforts by creating a cadre of volunteers and a proven donor base.

3. The organization has the desire, resources, and opportunity to manage a successful endowment campaign for a substantial amount of money. Since the money being raised in an endowment campaign is to be invested for future income, the goal should never be small. The effort required for an endowment campaign is too great to justify a result that when invested will yield only a few thousand dollars of yearly income.

Endowment campaigns ought to be rare creatures. They probably should have a separation of at least five or seven years between them. Special anniversary years of an organization's founding—the 10th, 25th, 50th—are often used to whip up interest, but an endowment campaign is not something that should be scheduled as regularly as every five years. You have to be careful about arbitrarily deciding that it's time to go out and make another pass at raising endowment. Like capital campaigns, endowment campaigns rely heavily upon large gifts from a few donors. Run them too close together, and you may find that your donor base is still meeting its last pledge. That does not bode well for the success of new requests.

While an annual campaign is a broad-based effort relying on smaller gifts from a great number of donors to achieve its goal, an endowment campaign expects a much smaller number of donors to make very large gifts. In an endowment campaign you should expect to get a third or more of the goal from 10 or 15 donors. The second third or more would then come from an additional 75 to 100 donors, and the remainder in smaller gifts from whatever other donor base you have targeted for the campaign. In short, *an endowment campaign must be a large-giver campaign.*

All too often, organizations that have decided on an endowment campaign begin with the idea of making it a broad-based appeal. You can't raise a million dollars by targeting as your primary donors those who have the capability to give $100 or even $1,000. You would have to identify 10,000 of the former or 1,000 of the latter. Rather, you need to begin by targeting prospects who can give $50,000—and remember, a number of those prospects may give only $5,000, or $10,000, or $20,000 instead of the $50,000 you have suggested.

At the Cleveland Orchestra, I once disagreed with the volunteer leadership of a $15-million endowment campaign about the size of gifts we should be seeking. The idea was put forth that we raise $5 million by enticing people to endow each of the 2,000 seats in Severance Hall. That worked out to $2,500 per donor. I went to the mat over this, literally risking my job. My reasoning was simple: We would not succeed in finding 2,000 donors at $2,500 each. Experience had shown me that the base of donors able and willing to give that much wasn't large enough. At best we would raise $1.5 million that way and as a result would fall short of our overall $15 million goal by $3.5 million, even if all other aspects of the campaign worked perfectly. I also feared that the campaign committee and solicitors would get used to the idea of asking small, and the campaign would lose its steam.

Thankfully my argument held, and the volunteer leadership agreed not to put so much of the campaign effort into an idea that past experience showed could not succeed without damaging other areas of the drive. In our effort to find 2,000 donors willing and able to make gifts of $2,500 we would have included donors we knew to be capable of making far larger gifts. These would be donors we would need to solicit for other, larger-gift divisions of the campaign. It is never a good idea to ask for two separate gifts for the same campaign. Donors will often make the decision to give either one or the other, and the option they pick can well be the lower.

Because of the amount of money being raised and the size of the gifts being sought, volunteer leadership and solicitors in an endowment campaign will be drawn more heavily from the upper echelons of the community's business and civic leaders. This fact, combined with the infrequency of endowment campaigns, gives them a far higher visibility than annual campaigns. An annual campaign which comes up a little short can often be glossed over. An endowment campaign which fails to make its goal—especially if that shortfall is substantial—invites questions about an organization's vitality, management, and potential for longevity. It also reflects badly on the campaign's highly visible volunteer leadership. People do not volunteer to lead fund-raising campaigns in order to fail publicly. An organization that begins an endowment campaign with a goal that does not match the capability of prospects to give dooms that campaign to failure, and organizations that experience a highly visible failure find it harder to recruit campaign leaders and solicitors for future efforts.

Endowment campaigns are of longer duration than annual campaigns. It takes more time to make the contacts and cultivate them, and it usually takes longer for donors to decide to give larger sums of money. My experience has been that, from kickoff to finish—no matter what the goal—an endowment campaign will last from 12 to 16 months. It is possible to wrap things up sooner, but the process should not be stretched much beyond a year and a quarter. An endowment campaign that lasts longer runs the risk of extending over two annual campaigns, and a seemingly endless endowment campaign can damage both the enthusiasm of an organization's volunteer base and its credibility with donors.

Two problems typically plague the start of endowment campaigns. One is deciding the amount of money to be ascribed to naming opportunities, and the other is the campaign brochure.

Many times endowment campaigns will be general in nature, seeking donations which will provide income for support. However, you can still create and offer commemorative naming opportunities. Other campaigns are for the purpose of endowing a specific project, position, program, etc., and as such offer explicit naming opportunities. As membership categories in an annual campaign work to suggest contribution levels, so do naming opportunities for endowment and capital campaigns. Naming faculty chairs, artistic positions, medical departments, buildings, and so on allows an organization to establish a tangible reward for a major contribution. This is especially bolstering to solicitors. It gives them something to "sell." The reason a donor gives should be to benefit the organization, but a naming opportunity, such as the Joe Smith Professor of Physics Chair, can be a great incentive for giving. However, naming opportunities do not always have to be taken as absolutely literal. Let me give you an example.

Many years back, the Cleveland Orchestra decided to conduct a campaign to endow all 17 of its principal chairs—first violin, second violin, first cello, and so on. The endowment raised would help the Orchestra attract and retain the finest players in the world. Each chair would be named for the person giving the endowment. Our primary goal, of course, was to raise money, but we also wanted to be the first orchestra in the country to endow all our principal chairs. If we had treated the concept of endowing a chair literally for its worth, we would have had to raise enough money to create sufficient endowment to provide income equal to each of the 17 musicians' then current salary and to allow for enough reinvestment to keep up with salary increases. Our assessment was that it would require $500,000 per chair to do this.

After rating and evaluating our prospects, we saw that we had only enough potential half-million-dollar donors to "literally" and completely endow only seven of the chairs. We did seem to have sufficient named-opportunity prospects to endow every chair at the $250,000 level. After much discussion we opted to take that route. The Cleveland Orchestra became the first symphony in the country to endow all its principal chairs, and we raised more money by lowering the requested amount than if we had completely endowed only those chairs for which we could find gifts of $500,000. An important point here, though, is that the amount we did seek, $250,000, was appropriate for the naming opportunity. This was not a fire sale; we did not give the chairs away.

Amazingly, one of the biggest challenges for endowment campaigns seems to be the creation of a suitable printed piece that presents the argument for the campaign. I have seen endowment campaigns actually languish and die because the organization could not come to agreement over design, number of pages, color, and phraseology. I believe this kind of impasse occurs more with endowment than annual campaigns because an endowment campaign is a very special event. Because it is not repeated every year, the previous year's material isn't there to serve as a model in developing a new brochure. Also, the nature of an endowment sometimes engenders among campaign leadership and volunteers an inordinately great fear of not being adequately prepared to ensure success.

Campaign management should make decisions about the brochure and other similar matters early on and stick to those decisions. Documents and strategy should not be continually revised in an attempt to obtain the complete agreement of everyone involved on each and every point. Consensus is important to achieve in fund-raising, but consensus does not mean you give 20 members of a campaign committee veto power over the color, size of type, or choice of words used in printed support material.

What I am saying about endowment campaigns also applies to capital campaigns, but there is one big difference. Endowment money raised is going to be invested in order to produce future income to fund future, not fully defined, endeavors. Capital campaigns are for a closely defined and tangible purpose. Campaign leadership and volunteer solicitors know exactly where the money is going. They can even show pictures of it.

CHAPTER 10

Capital Campaigns: Building for Now

A capital campaign raises money that will be spent to acquire or improve a physical asset. The most common use of a capital campaign is for the purchase, construction, or renovation of a building (commonly referred to as "bricks and mortar"). However, an organization can conduct a capital campaign to purchase machinery, equipment, furniture, fixtures, or any physical asset that can be reflected on its balance sheet.

The purpose of a capital campaign differs from that of an endowment campaign in that the money raised will not be used to cover ongoing, operational expenses, or to fund special projects. Capital funds are spent on one-time or seldom recurring expenditures. The primary difference between capital and endowment funds is that capital funds are not retained and invested to yield income. However, capital and endowment campaigns are very similar in their planning and management.

Like endowment campaigns, capital campaigns should be rare. The answer to the question of how frequently to conduct a capital campaign should lie within the organization's strategic plan. If an organization has successfully mapped out its growth, it can anticipate the points at which capital expenses will be incurred. In other words, need and planned strategy will determine when an organization should conduct a capital campaign. Frequent capital campaigns can sap the strength of an organization's annual fund campaign program. Keep going back to supporters with one special campaign on the heels of another, and sooner or later it will affect giving to the annual campaign. It is usually best if a number of years pass between the execution of two capital campaigns or between an endowment campaign and a capital campaign.

Capital campaigns should always aim to raise a substantial amount of money; the effort required is too great to justify raising money for an expense that, with a little planning and extra work, could be covered by annual operating funds. If the item you need to purchase is relatively low in cost, get the money for it by increasing your annual campaign goal.

Like endowment campaigns, *capital campaigns must be large-giver campaigns*. The same rule of thumb applies: Plan on raising one-third of the goal from 10 to 15 donors, a second third from an additional 75 to 100 donors, and the final third from the rest. All the arguments against broad-based endowment campaigns are just as potent when it comes to capital campaigns.

Because they rely heavily on large gifts to raise a substantial amount of money, capital campaigns draw their volunteer leadership and solicitors from the upper end of a community's business and civic leadership. The high visibility of a capital campaign ups the ante considerably. Few situations are more damaging to the image of an organization than announcing the planned construction of a new facility and then failing to raise the money to build.

Because of its substantial goal and small number of large donors, rating and evaluating prospects is extremely important in a capital campaign, which leads us to the most common mistake made in capital campaigns: setting a goal that is not reasonable. The motivating force for a capital campaign is the cost of the asset to be acquired. All too often, organizations make that cost figure the goal of the campaign without evaluating their donor base. It does no good to set a goal of $1 million if your donor base can provide, under the best of circumstances, only $500,000. *You have to make the decision to commit to a capital expense based on your ability to raise the money to pay for it, not decide how much money you need to raise based on the expense.* It is vitally important not to let the tail wag the dog.

Capital campaigns run longer than annual campaigns. Usually they should be wrapped up within a year, eliminating the risk of carrying over into successive annual campaigns. Ideally, the money to pay for a building should be in hand before the finish of the building. Actually, I suppose the ideal would be to have it in hand before ground-breaking. On the other hand, a ground-breaking is a wonderful fund-raising event, and taking prospective donors to a construction site or showing them the building to be purchased can be particularly compelling. There is, however, a very real risk in going too far with construction. If the building is completed and occupied, and the organization is trying to raise money to pay off a bridge loan, a campaign will have lost some of its sense of immediacy. It is also likely that by that time prospects will assume the campaign is over. After all, the organization has already moved into the building, hasn't it?

Since you are raising money that needs to be spent *now*, you will want to encourage cash gifts over deferred giving. With a deferred gift the organization is either given the promise of money or an asset to come at some predetermined time in the future, or it is given money or an asset now, with the understanding that it remain untouched by the organization so that the asset can earn income or provide some other benefit for the donor until some future date or event, such as the donor's demise. While the offer of a deferred gift poses no problem other than timing to those seeking to build an organization's endowment fund, fund-raisers seeking cash for capital projects should be ready with a plan for accepting deferred gifts. Ideally, when a prospect says, "I would love to help, but I really need the income from these assets to live on at this time," the solicitor needs to be able to say, "We have a deferred giving program. Let me show you how it works." At the very least the solicitor needs to be able to arrange for a meeting with the organization's deferred giving expert.

You take what you can get, and in the case of a bricks-and-mortar campaign, there may be a way to turn that deferred gift into endowment funds to help with the future expense of maintaining the building. Building an endowment fund into a bricks-and-mortar campaign is a good idea. Endowment reduces the pressure on future annual campaigns to raise the additional operating and maintenance money that will be needed to maintain the new facility.

Bricks-and-mortar capital campaigns also offer naming opportunities. In fact, naming opportunities are potentially an even stronger draw here than in endowment campaigns. Having your name on a building, a research laboratory, a lecture hall, or a treatment center can be even more gratifying than endowing a professorship or a chair in an orchestra. Again, as in endowment campaigns, a donor need not necessarily cover the entire expense of a new facility in order to be offered a naming opportunity. When a potential donor is considering making a gift that is far and away the largest donation to a bricks-and-mortar campaign and when that gift is truly a substantial portion—probably more than half—of the total expense of construction, then offering naming rights may be both appropriate and persuasive.

Another kind of gift that should be solicited during a bricks-and-mortar campaign is in-kind goods and services. If you need paint, why not ask a paint company to donate it? The company is likely to give you more paint than dollars to buy paint. Although organizations would generally rather have cash than any other kind of gift, capital campaigns are one of the few instances where there is no difference between cash and in-kind gifts. Just remember to give public credit for the cash value of an in-kind gift. The IRS won't let the donor deduct that amount, but you should publicly acknowledge what the gift was worth to the organization—what it would have cost "retail."

CHAPTER 11

Sponsorships and Underwriting Campaigns: Would You Please Fund Our ____?

Sponsorships and underwriting are different labels for basically the same thing: funding donated for the support of a project, program, event, initiative, activity, or even a salary. In general, foundations are identified as underwriters and corporations as sponsors. Individuals can be either, but in most instances underwriters and sponsors will be foundations and corporations.

The amount of publicity and recognition also helps answer the question of whether a funder is an underwriter or a sponsor. The word *sponsor* connotes a higher level of participation and consequently higher visibility than does *underwriter.* If one of the benefits a funder is seeking in exchange for support is publicity and recognition, then that funder is best identified as a sponsor. In very low visibility situations such as the funding of a position—an executive director, for instance—we would probably refer to the donor as an underwriter, even if the donor was a corporation. In the end it doesn't really matter whether you call a funding opportunity underwriting or sponsorship. Do what seems natural, what is usual within your community, and always do what the funder wants. If a corporation would rather be named an underwriter than a sponsor, then it's an underwriter.

For the purposes of this discussion, I will use the labels sponsor and sponsorship in instances where we could be talking about either a corporation or a foundation. Only when I wish to restrict the application of what I am saying to a foundation will I use the labels underwriter and underwriting.

Sponsorship, especially corporate sponsorship, is a relatively recent fund-raising strategy. I first began to see sponsorships with any frequency at all in the early 1980s. However, we can draw parallels between sponsorship and other fund-raising endeavors. A sponsorship campaign is like a capital campaign, for example, in that it raises money for a specific purpose. Unlike a capital campaign, however, the money raised is not used to purchase an asset, but rather to cover an expense. Like a capital campaign, sponsorships can provide naming opportunities—the ABC Corporation Lecture Series or the XYZ, Inc. Neighborhood Improvement Program, for instance. Sponsorship opportunities such as these often grow out of an organization's annual budgeting process, allowing it to pay for things it would have done even if a sponsor hadn't risen to the bait of a naming opportunity. These sponsorships permit an organization to package a need, in effect, as a means of boosting its annual support. The idea is to give greater credit and visibility to a sponsor in exchange for an increased contribution.

At one end of what I call the *sponsorship spectrum* are the donors who provide an organization's bedrock annual support. It makes sense to give these donors as much recognition and credit as possible. If their gifts are of a size to warrant, you can even specify that certain programs, efforts, or activities have been made possible because of their support. Once an organization has made a practice of linking gifts from certain donors to certain of its activities, the next step is to offer those donors sponsorships. Ideally, a single donor becomes the sole sponsor of an activity. The activity may be new, or already in existence. The sponsor gets the exclusive benefit of associating its name with the event or program. Often a sponsor's name can become synonymous with an event. When I say Thanksgiving Day parade, I bet the name Macy's jumps to mind. In a survey some years back, 97 percent of the participants made that association.

The beauty of funding something in this way is that you can ask for more money for a sponsorship than the donor was contributing to your annual fund-raising campaign. You can also ratchet up the cost of the sponsorship every few years: One that was available for $20,000 three or four years ago now requires a $25,000 contribution.

At the other end of the sponsorship spectrum are the companies and individuals who have shown no interest in your organization in the past. They may even have turned down earlier solicitations. A named sponsorship opportunity that provides high visibility can be just the ticket to drawing in a prospect who has previously been reluctant to give.

The first step in seeking sponsorships is to identify likely projects, programs, events, initiatives, and activities. I can't think of an organization that would not be bursting with underwriting or sponsorship opportunities. Remember, creating a sponsorship often requires nothing more than a rethinking of the means by which you fund something. Nearly any discrete endeavor can be pulled from a general budget and packaged for sponsorship.

Finding the best opportunities for sponsorship campaigns requires fund-raisers to "mine" their organization by looking hard at what activities are planned. Fund-raisers should meet regularly with senior staff to keep abreast of developments and to solicit their opinions about which activities might be viable for sponsorship. Once a sponsorship opportunity has been identified, a full-fledged proposal needs to be developed. This should include a budget, a case for giving which shows how the community and the organization will benefit, and a complete explanation of how the sponsor will benefit from the relationship.

Next comes the rating and evaluating of prospects. The goal is to narrow the field to the single best candidate and a handful of backups. A standing sponsorship committee of the board of trustees can be a great aid here and provide better leadership of this task than a committee formed separately for each sponsorship project.

Committee members, other fund-raisers, and organization management should keep well informed about both the kinds of endeavors that area foundations are willing to underwrite and which corporations are likely to be attracted to a sponsorship opportunity. That means staying on top of local and national business news. A firm that may have shown no past interest in supporting your organization (or any other, for than matter) can suddenly find itself needing the recognition and publicity a sponsorship opportunity can deliver. A marketing or public relations agency can be a useful advisor for identifying potential sponsors, and an organization should try to involve such a firm on a volunteer basis or perhaps even hire such services.

Once a sponsorship opportunity has been identified, a general proposal has been developed, and a candidate or candidates have been identified, the proposal must be tailored to fit each prospective donor. In this age of desktop publishing it is easy to produce a professional-looking prospectus targeted to each sponsorship candidate.

In general, sponsorship solicitations should be sequential. Only rarely, if ever, would you offer a sponsorship opportunity to two or more prospects at the same time. The danger is that more than one will accept. However, if the sponsorship is one of a number of similar opportunities, then one prospective sponsor may be able to be moved. If the organization is offering a unique named opportunity, then having to go back to a donor who has accepted the offer and say that you gave it to someone else has the potential for permanently damaging that relationship.

However, each sponsorship opportunity is its own campaign, and you can undertake several sponsorship campaigns simultaneously with other fund-raising campaigns.

You would do well to allow as much time as possible for a sponsorship campaign. Even a turndown takes time, and a sponsored endeavor usually has a "drop-dead" date—the point after which it becomes impossible to recognize and publicize a donation and include the donor in sponsorship publications such as brochures, schedules, and programs and in activities such as dinners, cocktail parties, and openings. Fund-raisers need to plan backward from the drop-dead date in order to allow time to solicit more than one potential sponsor if that becomes necessary.

Sponsorship campaigns have no ideal length, and because they are conducted behind the scenes, they can go on for as long as it takes to elicit a positive response, or until the drop dead-date has passed. The invisibility of this kind of campaign means that failure causes little real damage, other than the missing funding. Since failure in a sponsorship campaign is "private" and there is no hard-and-fast time frame beyond the final drop-dead date, organizations need to be very careful about not letting sponsorship opportunities slip away. Sponsorships need to be pursued with the same vigor as annual, endowment, and capital campaigns.

Perhaps the most common mistake made in a sponsorship campaign is to let ancillary expenses rise by making overly generous commitments to the sponsor. Corporate sponsors are particularly likely to suggest expenses which are covered by the sponsor's gift but which are not part of the sponsored endeavor's regular budget. Items which the sponsor may ask for as part of its benefit package can include, but are not restricted to:

1. Advertising
2. Parties and other free entertainment for customers, clients, and employees
3. Hundreds of free tickets, which could otherwise be sold, to an event
4. Special publications, posters, and other printed materials
5. Elaborate press functions

There is a tendency on the part of fund-raisers to promise special considerations to sponsors. That inclination must be resisted, but with as much tact as possible. Out-of-pocket expenses can destroy the value of a sponsorship donation if they are allowed to get out of hand.

A sponsored endeavor that does not meet the organization's or the sponsor's expectations poses another potential danger. Neither foundations, nor corporations, nor individuals want to have their names attached to negative publicity. Controversial endeavors do not make good sponsorship opportunities. Be sure there is no hidden potential for controversy in those activities for which you seek sponsorship.

In my experience, the biggest problem fund-raisers are likely to encounter with sponsorships is that there is always somebody back at the shop—a staff member or trustee—who objects strenuously (and, to my mind, often unreasonably) to some of the benefits given in exchange for sponsorship. The impact of these objections can be diminished by having the key players clearly define in advance what courtesies and considerations will be extended to a sponsor. If a non-profit organization earns a portion of its income, then the people running the marketing operation need to be apprised of and in agreement with just how much of what they sell is—from their point of view—going to be "given away" to a sponsor. Good relations between an organization's fund-raisers and marketers are very important. They need to work together as a team to produce the income which is their common goal.

Then there is the person who feels it necessary to protect the sanctity of an organization against all commercial "defilement." No organization should compromise its mission or its integrity in search of funding. A sponsor is buying neither the organization nor the sponsored endeavor. However, it is acquiring some rights of association, recognition, and publicity. I recall with particular amazement an incident that happened some years ago at a policy meeting of a statewide arts funding council. Some idealistic person raised an objection to the proposal that the council's logo should be printed in the lower right corner of posters publicizing events or organizations the arts council had funded. The next thing I knew, the head of one of the largest arts organizations in the state was on his feet, saying, "That's a very good point, and most of us are really bothered by demands to use the *vulgar* logos of our sponsors." The collective gasp could have been heard in the next room. And this comment came from a person whose organization was in the middle of a mammoth sponsorship campaign.

On the other hand, it is important to remember that all donations, including sponsorships, are basically philanthropic in nature. What we do to recognize a sponsor's contribution is just that—recognition. Be careful how you tout the "market value" of sponsorship benefits. An organization should not look at a sponsorship as a quid pro quo arrangement with each contributed dollar buying additional benefit for the sponsor. All but the most inexperienced sponsors know they are making a donation. Don't work so hard to convince sponsors of the value they will receive that they cease to see their sponsorship as a philanthropic endeavor.

An organization mounts a sponsorship campaign in order to increase its donated income. Sponsorships are an effective way both of enlarging existing annual gifts and of drawing in new corporate donors. There are secondary benefits as well. One is the credibility to be gained when a company or foundation allows its name to be associated with that of the organization. This quite plainly and simply amounts to an endorsement, and the bigger the company or more highly regarded the foundation, the greater the impact of that endorsement. An organization establishes a richer, more complex relationship with a donor who is also a sponsor. In the case of corporate sponsors, this often leads middle- and upper-level corporate management to deeper involvement with the organization, resulting in the expansion of its volunteer base and the development of potential leaders for its fund-raising campaigns.

Often, one of the benefits extended to sponsors is a reception or entertainment event. When this happens the organization's trustees, administrators, and fund-raisers have the opportunity to rub shoulders with corporate executives and other invited guests. It is a chance to meet and get the ears of some of a community's most important people. Suddenly, you are sitting at a table with the company's CEO and spouse or the public relations VP and spouse, and that is a true networking opportunity.

CHAPTER 12

Developing a Campaign Plan

Every fund-raising campaign succeeds or fails largely on the strength of its planning. A campaign plan is the fund-raiser's road map, agenda, and explanation. It assesses campaign goals, develops strategies, and determines tactics. It delineates how much money is to be raised, by whom, using what means, in how much time, and for what purpose. A realistic fund-raising campaign cannot succeed without a well-drawn, fully conceived plan.

Planning is the most important part of any campaign. The person charged with an organization's overall fund-raising responsibility must, with the advice and assistance of staff and board, develop the plan, present it to the campaign's volunteer leadership, and oversee its implementation and execution. While some might think that involving the volunteer leadership of a campaign in the planning process is desirable and would result more readily in consensus, my experience suggests otherwise. Volunteer leadership is far more comfortable responding to a proposed game plan than to being asked to start from scratch. You won't get far by saying, "We need $50,000 by the end of the year, Mr. Jones. Now, how do you think we ought to raise it?"

Planning a fund-raising campaign is not hard to do, nor does it have to take a long time. It is a methodical process that just about anyone can accomplish by carrying out the following seven steps:

1. Settle on an achievable goal
2. Develop a case for support
3. Prepare a campaign funding projection
4. Decide what forms of solicitation to use
5. Develop a campaign calendar
6. Define the volunteer positions needed by type and number and write job descriptions for each
7. Prepare a publicity plan

Settling on an Achievable Goal

Planning for a fund-raising campaign begins with the recognition of a budgetary need—be it to offset an operational deficit, create an endowment, add a wing to a building, or fund a program. When an organization's executive director or board president says, "We need to raise $100,000 to cover _____," that number, $100,000, becomes the target of a campaign.

I say target and not goal because an achievable goal should be determined by assessing the amount that can be raised to meet the need. The fund-raising resources available to an organization are a reality against which the target should be measured for feasibility. Those resources consist of the volunteer leadership and solicitors available to work a campaign and a realistically rated and evaluated list of prospective donors. If the resources are insufficient to raise the money which the organization has targeted, there are only two options. Either the goal must be set lower than the target, at a level consistent with available resources, or the resources must be enlarged to meet a goal equal to the targeted need.

When target and resources are far apart, an organization's leadership will almost invariably decide that the former cannot be shrunk to a goal in line with the latter. In such a situation, the person responsible for creating the campaign plan must point out the paucity of resources and argue for a lesser goal. If that approach fails, the next step is to obtain the trustees' agreement to increase the resources. They will have to commit to finding more strong volunteers, to developing a longer list of prospective donors, and to providing the leadership needed to bring in larger amounts of money from each donor.

Developing a Case for Support

The case for support is the argument for the fund-raising campaign. It grows out of an organization's mission statement in the sense that the money to be raised will be used by the organization to support its mission. In the case of an annual fund campaign this relationship is obvious and direct and the case for support is by and large a statement of the organization's reason for being and the value of its contribution to the community. To this is added a sense of the immediacy of the current campaign—indications of what will be lost if the money is not raised or the danger to the vitality of the organization of failing to cover an operational deficit. In endowment, capital, and sponsorship campaigns, the case for support calls particular attention to the purpose of the campaign—what is to be funded—and its importance to the organization and the community.

Developing the case for support and settling on the goal of a campaign are preliminary, almost intuitive, steps in the process of creating a campaign plan, and they generally occur simultaneously. The goal is the overriding concern of the campaign, and the focus and strength of the case to be made for the campaign are dependent on the size and purpose of a goal. The case for support becomes the main tool used to recruit volunteer campaign leadership and solicitors and to convince prospective donors. It should be only a few sentences in length, easily understood, and readily able to be paraphrased by solicitors.

Sample Case for Support

The XYZ Institute has been serving our community for 20 years with programs that *(list and description of programs and activities that are central to the organization's mission)* **. Last year more than 20,000 people in our community directly benefited from our activities, and countless others receive the indirect benefit of living in a community where efforts such as ours improve the quality of life for all. Each year we go to corporations, foundations, and individuals in the community to raise money to help make up the difference between the fees we obtain and our mounting expenses. We rely on donors such as you to make possible our ongoing programs and services, and to enable us to undertake important new initiatives, such as** *(list and description of planned new programs and activities)* **. As you can see, the vital services we perform are made possible by the thoughtful generosity of supporters such as you. I sincerely hope you will be able to help us again with a gift this year.**

This model statement can easily be adapted to fit an endowment, capital, or sponsorship campaign by stressing the purpose of the specific campaign, explaining why the endowment or expenditure is necessary, delineating who will benefit from it and how, and calling attention to the immediacy of the fund-raising effort. It is not necessary to include every argument and all evidence in the basic case statement, but facts, figures, and a supportive array of anecdotal information should be readily available. These materials become part of the campaign's solicitation kit.

Preparing a Campaign Projection

A campaign projection shows how much money needs to be raised and the sources from which it will come. By allocating expectations by type of donor and size of gift, it becomes an available yardstick. The projection is the ideal against which the progress of the campaign is continuously plotted, allowing fund-raisers to see where they are meeting expectations and where they are falling behind. Using this information it is possible to make mid-course corrections or restructure a campaign to create a greater opportunity for success.

Sample Endowment or Capital Campaign Projection

Division	Goal	Percent of Total Goal
Individuals	$2,000,000	50.0
Foundations	1,100,000	27.5
Corporations	900,000	22.5
Total	**$4,000,000**	**100.0**

Number of Gifts	Size of Gifts	Percent of Total Goal
3	$500,000	37.5
4	250,000	25.0
8	100,000	20.0
10	50,000	12.5
12	25,000	7.5
163	Under 25,000	10.0
Total 200	**$4,000,000**	**100.0**

A campaign projection cannot be prepared without making some basic assumptions. In the foregoing example, it is assumed that rating and evaluation will provide enough prospects in each size-of-gift category to yield the anticipated number of gifts. Once again, this is a situation in which you start out with targets and then determine whether you have sufficient resources to turn those targets into achievable goals. If not, you must either lower the goal or increase your fund-raising resources.

You begin the assessment of resources by looking at what your last campaign brought in and who made it work. The more proven resources you have to start with, the fewer additional ones you will need to find. Therefore, it is crucially important to identify both experienced persons to work the current campaign and repeatable gifts. In the case of an annual campaign that is being repeated, you should look at the previous year's record and ask these questions:

1. Who is available from the last campaign to step into a leadership role this year?
2. How many of last year's solicitors and solicitation team captains are available to work this year?
3. How many of last year's major donors have died?
4. How many of last year's major donors have moved out of town?
5. How many of last year's major donors are unlikely to be able to give at the same or a higher level this year?

In other words, you must look long and hard at what you raised the previous year and how much of that amount is repeatable. Let's say the goal this year is 20 percent higher than the previous year's result of $100,000. The total you will need to raise this year is $120,000. However, let's also say that 15 percent of the money raised the previous year simply isn't available because of attrition of your donor base. That means that instead of having to find an additional $20,000 of new money, you will have to produce $35,000 over what your proven donor base contributed the previous year.

The same process works, in modified form, for endowment, capital, and sponsorship campaigns. You may not find an exact model of the current campaign, but the organization, unless it is brand new, probably has some fund-raising history on which to fall back. Those persons who establish the target are basing, at least to some extent, their fund-raising assumptions on past performance or the performance of other nonprofit organizations within the community. When I walked through the door as the Cleveland Orchestra's first development director, my job was to understand the needs of the organization, determine what had been done in the past, and then do all I could to embellish and enlarge that past performance.

Deciding Which Forms of Solicitation to Use

There are many different techniques for communicating with prospects and requesting donations. My experience suggests the following to be the most efficient and effective:

1. One-on-one solicitation at a predetermined appointment
2. Door-to-door solicitation
3. Direct mail
4. Telefunding

One-on-one solicitation is the only way to obtain large gifts. There is no substitute for looking someone in the eye and asking for the money. Even in the case of corporations and foundations, it still comes down to one person talking with another.

A one-on-one solicitation for a larger gift requires a fair amount of planning. You can't just show up on the doorstep as you would in a door-to-door campaign. Generally it is best to begin by sending a letter that includes the case for giving and notification of an impending phone call to schedule an appointment. The letter should also note the amount previously contributed (if applicable), and the suggested size of gift. Including the amount of the suggested gift in this proposal letter lets the prospect know what to expect. Just as important, it gets everything out on the table for the solicitor. Many solicitors have a hard time asking for a suggested gift amount. In fact, they can be so uncomfortable with the thought of doing so that their discomfiture hovers, like a black cloud, over the entire meeting. Obviously, this does not create an atmosphere conducive to making a good presentation. Putting the suggested gift size in the letter eliminates this worry and distraction for the solicitor.

My general recommendation that the amount of the desired gift should be indicated in letters and proposals, while effective in most cases, is not suitable in all instances, especially when the gift sought is extremely large and the relationship with the prospect is not close. In those situations, or whenever in doubt, just use the letter or proposal to provide campaign information and to make the case, and state your intent to discuss the matter further in person. Thus, your presentation of the suggested asking amount will occur later in the solicitation process. Sometimes the amount of the contribution sought can be discreetly pointed out without being specifically mentioned by sending a list of named gift opportunities or the organization's membership information along with a letter in which it is suggested that the prospect consider endowing a certain position or program or joining the _____ Society at a certain level. The enclosed documentation will clearly specify the amount you desire the prospect to see and consider.

One-on-one solicitation is the most important element of the actual campaign. It is the only way that large gifts can be successfully solicited, and it is also the best way to bring in the smaller gifts. In the next chapter, when we look at the components of a solicitor's kit, you will see how much effort goes into prepping solicitors to ask a prospect for the money.

Door-to-door solicitation is another form of one-on-one asking. Usually done without an appointment, this technique is used in campaigns seeking broad public support and small gifts. Fund-raisers who can manage the administration of a door-to-door campaign will find it to be very lucrative. The administrative headaches come from the need to recruit a very large base of volunteer solicitors and to prepare them to knock on doors. The most effective door-to-door solicitors are persons whom the prospect will recognize either by sight or name. At the very least they must be able to say, "I live down the block." For door-to-door to work optimally, it is crucial that the solicitors work their own neighborhoods. Also, door-to-door solicitation needs to be conducted face-to-face, with the solicitor standing before the prospect and making the case for support. An envelope left in the mailbox or hung on the door won't do the job nearly as well and, in fact, differs very little from direct mail.

Direct mail is best used as a cold approach to prospects who have no identifiable relationship with the organization. It is a way to reach people who are not part of a constituency of an organization. For example, I would use direct mail to solicit prospects whose names have been acquired from other organizations or a mailing list house. Some people may feel that direct mail is the best way to contact large numbers of people who have a "consumer" relationship with an organization—ticket buyers. I don't. You may want to send them a piece telling about the campaign and presenting the case for support, but that should be followed up with a telephone call to ask for the money. One human being speaking to another who has a relationship with the organization will bring in far more money than a brochure, letter, and return envelope.

Telefunding is a technique that over the past decade has grown tremendously in popularity, as it works relatively well with a constituency of an organization. However, because of the sheer number of organizations, both profit and non-profit, engaging in telephone sales and solicitations, a noticeable resistance, even a hostility, to "sales" phone calls has sprung up among callees who see callers as uninvited invaders of home or place of work. Combine that with the fact that solicitor and prospect are not making eye contact, and it becomes far easier for a prospect to say no. All a prospect needs to do is hang up the phone, with or without the usual courtesies, as anyone who has ever used the phone to ask for donations or sell something knows.

The logistics of phone solicitation can also be daunting. A hard-working solicitor can complete about 10 full solicitations per hour. The window of time available to make calls to a person's home is only about two and a half hours in the evening, roughly from 6:00 until 8:30 p.m. If an organization has 10 available phone lines, 2,000 phone solicitations will take a minimum of eight evenings under optimal conditions.

Phone solicitation does have some advantages. Volunteers who feel uncomfortable asking someone for money face-to-face often turn into real pros on the phone. Protected from embarrassment by the anonymity of the telephone and able to have crib notes in front of them, they feel more relaxed and thus find it easier to ask for money. Also, phone solicitation can be fairly inexpensive. Especially if an organization gets a company to donate the use of its offices and phones in the evening hours as headquarters for its volunteer callers.

However, unless the callers are representing an organization about which the prospect cares, they are unlikely to meet with a very warm reception. I would use telefunding only with a constituency of an organization or with persons who know or are able to identify the person making the call, but not as an approach to those unlikely to have knowledge of either the organization or the solicitor.

Developing a Campaign Calendar

We have previously discussed the ideal length for each type of campaign. Now let's talk about the events that make up a fund-raising campaign and the optimal time they should occur.

The campaign calendar delineates the timing of meetings, kickoffs, events, press releases, money-raised milestones, celebrations, and just about anything else that it is anticipated will happen during a campaign. It is the time line of a campaign and another yardstick used to measure progress. It is a schedule of deadlines.

On the opposite page is a typical campaign calendar, displayed as a time line over a seven-month period starting at the point at which it is decided to have a fund-raising campaign and running through the final review of the campaign. I have used the time line format to more clearly show the progression of events. However, the actual calendar prepared for the campaign is probably better set up as a list of deadlines, tasks, and events to be checked off as they are met or occur.

Defining the Volunteers' Jobs

The first position that needs to be defined in a fund-raising campaign is that of the chair of a campaign. This person is the linchpin of the campaign. It is the chair who recruits others for leadership positions, sets the tone for the campaign, opens doors to major givers, and, when necessary, cracks the whip.

Campaign Chair Job Description

The campaign chair's first major responsibility is to recruit a committee consisting of the chairs of the major divisions of the campaign, other needed leadership, and, if needed, a co-chair. The campaign chair leads the committee in rating and evaluating major prospects already known to the organization; in identifying, rating, and evaluating major new prospects; and in setting appointments with major prospects and soliciting their donations. The campaign chair has overall responsibility for executing the campaign plan and functions as the campaign's chief operating officer, running scheduled meetings of the campaign volunteer

SAMPLE ANNUAL FUND CAMPAIGN CALENDAR

JANUARY	Develop goal, plan, and case for support by January 5 Recruit campaign chair by January 30
FEBRUARY	Recruit division chairs by February 13
MARCH	Recruit team captains and solicitors by March 6 Identify, rate, and evaluate prospects by March 13 Develop solicitation kit and prepare publicity plan by March 27
APRIL	Hold campaign kickoff meeting on April 5 Issue press release announcing start of campaign on April 10
MAY	Hold first progress meeting on May 3 Issue campaign newsletter on progress on May 8 Hold second progress meeting on May 31
JUNE	Issue campaign newsletter on progress on June 5 Hold final progress meeting on June 28
JULY	Issue campaign newsletter on progress on July 6 Close campaign on July 28 Issue final newsletter and press release on July 31

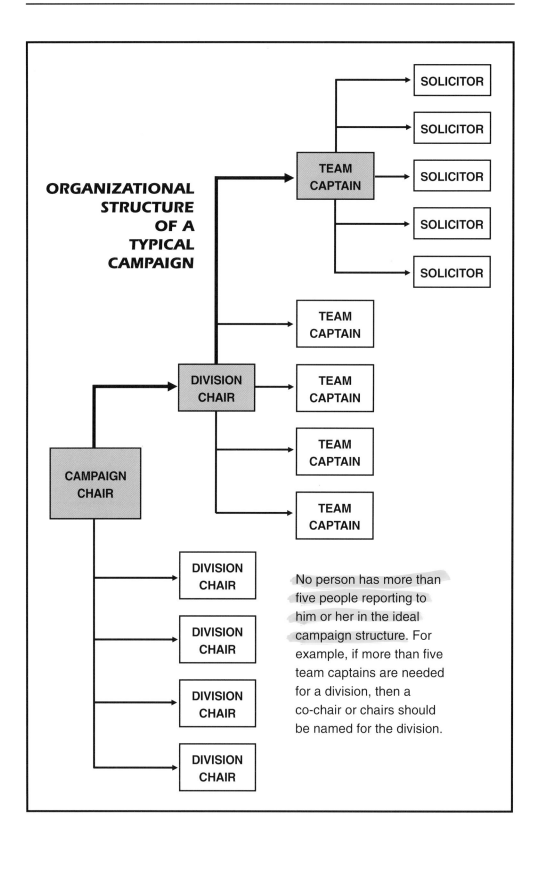

ORGANIZATIONAL STRUCTURE OF A TYPICAL CAMPAIGN

SOLICITOR

SOLICITOR

SOLICITOR

SOLICITOR

SOLICITOR

TEAM CAPTAIN

TEAM CAPTAIN

TEAM CAPTAIN

TEAM CAPTAIN

TEAM CAPTAIN

TEAM CAPTAIN

DIVISION CHAIR

CAMPAIGN CHAIR

DIVISION CHAIR

DIVISION CHAIR

DIVISION CHAIR

DIVISION CHAIR

No person has more than five people reporting to him or her in the ideal campaign structure. For example, if more than five team captains are needed for a division, then a co-chair or chairs should be named for the division.

team and calling additional meetings as needed. The campaign chair is the public spokesperson for the campaign, making statements to the media and urging participation on the part of prospective donors. The campaign chair reports to the chair of the board of trustees.

After the campaign chair in the hierarchy of volunteers come the chairs of the campaign divisions. In annual, capital, and endowment campaigns, the effort is usually broken into at least five divisions:

1. Major corporate and business gifts
2. Smaller corporate and business gifts
3. Foundations
4. Major individual gifts
5. Smaller individual gifts

Each of these divisions may be divided further according to your needs. Corporate and individual givers are separated by size of gift, while foundations, because there are usually far fewer of them, are treated as a single group. In dealing with corporations it is important to categorize by size of the desired gift, not by the size of corporation, for it is not necessarily the largest corporations who will make the biggest gifts.

Division Chair Job Description

The division chair's initial major responsibility is to recruit a cadre of persons who will function as solicitation team captains and, if needed, a co-chair. The division chair has management responsibility for all fund-raising efforts within the division. He or she assists the team captains in recruiting solicitors, runs scheduled division meetings, calls additional meetings as needed, assists in contacting and soliciting prospects, and keeps the campaign chair informed of the division's progress. The division chair reports to the campaign chair or co-chair.

Solicitation team captains are the taskmasters of a fund-raising campaign. They see that the actual work of soliciting prospects gets done in a timely manner.

Solicitation Team Captain Job Description

The solicitation team captain's first major responsibility is to recruit a team of five or six solicitors. The team captain has responsibility for

managing the team, seeing that all prospects are contacted and solicited in accordance with the campaign plan and schedule; assisting solicitors in their efforts; and keeping the division chair informed of the team's progress. The team captain reports to a division chair or co-chair.

Solicitors make the vast majority of requests. They are the frontline salespeople of a fund-raising campaign.

Solicitor Job Description

The solicitor's primary responsibilities are to contact assigned prospects, present the case for support, answer questions, and request a suggested donation. Ideally, a solicitor will be assigned five prospects. The solicitor reports to the team captain and keeps him or her informed of progress.

In the ideal campaign no more than five persons report to any position, which is why we make provision for vice-chairs at the campaign and division chair levels. Although there will be exceptions to this rule, keep in mind that campaign leaders and solicitors are volunteers. The fund-raising campaign is not their only priority. Never saddle a volunteer with an excessive amount of work or management responsibility.

Preparing a Publicity Plan

Publicity can be a very useful tool during a fund-raising campaign, especially in the case of a broad-based effort that is reaching out to the general public. An organization seeks publicity for a campaign to create an awareness of the organization's value to the community and the financial need that has brought about the campaign. This heightened awareness will assist in creating a climate conducive to giving. A secondary reason for publicizing a campaign is to give recognition to the efforts of volunteers, particularly the campaign's leaders.

A publicity plan is nothing more than the scheduling of announcements and events at intervals which will work to achieve the above goal. Opportunities for publicity need to be scheduled in advance and noted in the campaign calendar so that plans actually get carried out once the campaign is under way. Too often, good intentions are swept away in the onrush of activities in a campaign. Writing and mailing a press release become tasks that the fund-raiser will "get around to" when there is a break in the activity.

Actually, most campaign press releases can be written prior to the campaign kickoff, with names and numbers to be inserted at a future time. Just remember that all public statements should emanate from a single spokesperson, usually the campaign chair.

What events can be scheduled as publicity getters? Here is a list of the most common:

1. Naming of campaign chair and goal
2. Campaign kickoff with civic endorsements
3. First major gift
4. Twenty-five percent of goal reached
5. Fifty percent of goal reached
6. Seventy-five percent of goal reached
7. Major gifts received (as appropriate)
8. Ground-breaking (in the case of a capital campaign)
9. Ninety percent of goal reached
10. Goal reached

You should also be on the alert for publicity opportunities that simply aren't expected.

A good publicity effort requires that someone take responsibility for its execution. A fund-raiser's job is to raise money. If a fund-raiser gets sidetracked by the search for publicity, the campaign itself can be placed in jeopardy. Publicity must be kept in its place. In fact, it is best left to the communications or marketing departments of an organization or a volunteer communications professional. It is their job, after all, and the smart fund-raiser asks that they generate the required publicity, leaving the fund-raisers to work on the real job—achieving the campaign goal.

CHAPTER 13

Preparing for a Campaign: Assembling the People and the Tools to Ask for the Money

Once the campaign plan has been developed, the organization knows what it wants to do and how it plans to do it. Still to be determined is who will be recruited to do what and the kit of materials which they will be given to assist them in making their requests.

Recruiting Campaign Leadership and Solicitors

Sometimes, recruitment of the chair of a campaign occurs simultaneously with the development of the campaign plan, and in some instances the chair is involved in the planning process. However, it is best to contact a prospective chair with a job description and a campaign plan in hand. There are two distinct advantages to proceeding in this order. First, control of the planning process is left in the hands of the person who has responsibility for raising an organization's contributed income. Presumably, this person is a professional development officer or has extensive fund-raising knowledge and experience. Such a person should be better equipped than the volunteer campaign leader to develop a realistic and effective plan.

The second advantage to having a plan prepared before recruiting a campaign chair is that it speeds the process of recruitment. A well-prepared plan shows a level of commitment and professionalism on the part of the organization that should be attractive to the person being recruited. It prevents a prospective chair from putting you off by saying, "It sounds good, but why don't you get back to me with a game plan, and then I'll take a hard look at doing it." Well-conceived campaign plans provide the information prospective chairs need to determine whether they have the desire and time to commit to a campaign.

The primary responsibility for recruiting a campaign chair falls to the chair of the organization's board of trustees. If he or she is unable to do it, then some other trustee should take the responsibility. If that is not feasible, then the organization's executive director must do the recruiting. In the ideal scenario, the board chair will collaborate with a standing trustee committee on development and the organization's executive director and its development officer to generate a short list of campaign chair candidates. From that list the standing committee on development working with the development officer will choose a prospective campaign chair. It is then up to the board chairperson or, if there is such, a trustee having a special relationship with the candidate to make the recruitment contact.

Often, a trustee of the organization will be recruited as the campaign chair. There are times, however, when someone other than a trustee may be better suited to run a campaign. The chair of a campaign needs to have leverage and clout proportionate to the amount of money to be raised. It is the chair who will recruit other key players and who is likely to be called on either to solicit or help solicit the largest donors. Even with a good plan, a campaign that has inappropriate or insufficient leadership will be doomed.

I once worked on a major capital campaign for an organization whose board members were good and dedicated people, but none had the stature within the community to raise several million dollars. Fortunately, they were able to recruit the CEO of a large bank to chair the campaign, even though he had no previous relationship with the organization.

Once a person has signed on to chair the campaign, he or she then recruits campaign division chairs and, if needed, a campaign co-chair. The division chairs then recruit the team captains, and the team captains recruit the solicitors. In each of these stages, the pool of recruits can come from the contacts of the person doing the recruiting or the organization's volunteer base (usually, it's a combination). However, the stronger the relationship between a campaign chair and the division chairs, between a division chair and the team captains, and between a team captain and the solicitors, the greater the likelihood of success, because the campaign will benefit from the team's interlocking feelings of personal loyalty and responsibility. The only weakness of teams organized along these lines occurs when there is a break in the chain. If the captain of a team of solicitors leaves town and no one on the team wants to step up and become captain, it is almost impossible to transfer responsibility for the team to a new captain and have it work at the same level of efficiency. Given the potentially positive results that can arise from encouraging volunteer campaign leaders to recruit the people who will report to them, it's worth risking that occasional downside.

Solicitation Kits

Solicitation kits are the support mechanism for solicitors in the field. When solicitors sit alone at the phone, preparing to call prospects for an appointment, all they have to fall back on for inspiration and guidance is the packet of materials they received at the campaign kickoff meeting. For this reason the solicitation kit must:

1. Instill confidence
2. Provide needed information
3. Be easy to use

The kit instills confidence by looking thoroughly professional and by providing data on other successful campaigns—reporting, for example, how much the annual campaign raised the previous year and explaining how the goal was achieved. It helps solicitors answer questions by supplying comprehensive background information on the organization and the current campaign. A solicitation kit is easy to use when it is well organized, contains support materials and tools designed for the current campaign, and eschews extraneous materials. There is a temptation to put every printed piece available into a solicitation kit.

"Do you think they can use this, Mary?"

"I'm not sure, Joe."

"Well, let's go ahead and put it in just in case."

Resist that temptation. A packed solicitation kit is not a useful tool. It requires solicitors to expend too much effort sorting the wheat from the chaff, and its sheer size can be intimidating.

The first step in organizing a solicitation kit is to understand that it has two parts: support materials and information needed by the solicitors and materials and information to be given to prospects. At a bare minimum a solicitation kit should include the following:

1. Case for support of the campaign
2. Most recent annual report of the organization or an executive summary of it
3. Campaign organization chart and list of volunteers
4. Solicitor job description
5. Campaign calendar
6. Profile and report form for each prospect, with contribution record and suggested giving level
7. One-page description of the organization, its value to the community, and its past successes

8. Additional support materials such as newspaper clippings, press releases, and awards received

9. Suggested proposal letter

10. Organization or campaign stationery

11. Pledge cards or gift envelopes

The first six of these items fall into the category of support materials and information that solicitors use to do their job. Items seven through eleven are materials and information that solicitors can put into the hands of prospects. Let's review each document separately.

We talked about the case for support and gave an example in the last chapter. An organization's most recent annual report contains information on recent accomplishments, a copy of the mission statement, and financial data.

A typical campaign committee organization chart should contain both position titles and the name of the person in each position and an alphabetical list of all participants in the campaign. Volunteers like to know who else is taking part, as such information can be useful to them during the campaign and later in social and business situations.

Examples of a job description for solicitors and a campaign calendar can be found in the previous chapter.

The prospect profile and report form is a one-page document which performs two functions. It first provides information about a prospect to the solicitor, and then becomes the solicitor's outcome report to campaign leadership. Solicitors should receive a profile of every prospect assigned to them that includes the following information:

1. Prospect's name and name of spouse when applicable

2. Prospect's address and day and evening phone numbers

3. Prospect's relationship to the organization (user of services, member, season ticketholder, former trustee, associate of a present trustee, etc.), when applicable

4. Prospect's employer and title

5. Prospect's past contributions to the organization

6. Prospect's suggested gift to the current campaign

7. Name of anyone who is available to assist in the solicitation and the form of their possible assistance

8. Suggested solicitation strategy or advice

The form should leave blanks for reporting the results of the solicitation, including the following information:

1. Solicitor's name and phone numbers

2. Dates of contacts and result of each contact

3. Checklist of documents presented to prospect (types of giving opportunities, pledge card, etc.)

4. Final results of solicitation, including amount given or pledged or reason for refusal

5. Next step (send thank-you, redeem pledge, etc.)

6. Additional comments which could be helpful for future solicitation efforts

The prospect profiles and report forms are the most important documents in a solicitation kit. On a single sheet of paper are the facts needed to prep solicitors for each contact and a place to record and report results. The more complete the data a solicitor is given, the greater will be the confidence level of the solicitor and the greater the likelihood of a successful solicitation. The more complete the solicitor's report, the stronger the organization's understanding will be of what happened during the solicitation and the better its data for future solicitations.

While prospect profile and report forms will vary somewhat in the information they contain and their appearance according to the dictates of the campaign, the concept of the form will remain the same. An example of a prospect profile and report form for a capital campaign is shown on page 78. It has been filled in and is ready to go back to campaign leadership.

The one-page description of the organization should be developed out of standing public relations material tailored to stress aspects which advance the current fund-raising campaign. Additional support materials can consist of pamphlets, newspaper clippings, letters of praise, documentation of awards, and so forth. Just about anything which shows the organization in a good light can be included.

A sample proposal letter should also be included in the solicitation kit. It should:

1. State the case for support of the fund-raising campaign

2. Cite the prospect's history of generosity, if there is one, to the organization

3. Mention the amount of the gift the organization is suggesting, if that tactic has been deemed appropriate for this prospect

4. Explain that the solicitor will be contacting the prospect to set up an appointment

Including the amount of the suggested gift in the proposal letter accomplishes two things. It prompts prospects to begin thinking about the size of their gift early in the process, and it eliminates any potential discomfort a solicitor may feel about having to introduce the suggested gift in person.

Often the proposal letter is sent out over the signature of the chair of the campaign or that of a division chair. In those instances the proposal letter is included in the

Capital Campaign Prospect Profile and Report Form

Prospect Profile

Prospect's name _____ Joe Smith _____   **Spouse** _____ Mary _____

Address _____ 555 Hillside Ave., New City, OH 00000 _____

Business phone _____ 555-5555 _____   **Home phone** _____ 666-6666 _____

Employer _____ Amalgamated Corp. _____   **Title** _____ VP Research _____

Relationship to XYZ Institute _____ Grandson of former trustee _____

Contribution summary Has made contribution to annual campaign for past ten years: 1995— $1,000 1994—$1,000, 1993—$800, 1992—$700, 1991—$500. Contributed $5,000 to 1990 endowment campaign.

Solicitation assistance Bob Clarke, campaign chair, will send solicitation proposal letter on May 12 with copy to you.

Solicitation strategy & advice Remind him that Amalgamated Corp. is a very active supporter and that the chairman of Amalgamated, Bill Wilson, is a former president of our board.

Suggested gift _____ $10,000

Solicitor's Report

Solicitor's name _____ Gary Jones _____

Business phone _____ 777-7777 _____   **Home phone** _____ 888-8888 _____

Contact dates and results May 15: phoned and got appointment for May 20. May 17: got call to reschedule appointment to May 23. May 23: made solicitation. He said he would have to talk it over with wife. May 27: phoned to see where things were, he said still had to talk to wife but set appointment for June 3. June 3: he pledged $10,000.

Have I: **Suggested multiyear (to five years) pledge**   ✓

Suggested named gift opportunities   ✓

Presented the pledge card   ✓

Results: **Pledge amount** $10,000

Decision pending   _____

Why refused _____

Next step _____ Send thank-you _____

Additional comments He is getting a promotion next month to Sr. VP Research & Product Development. Probably substantial pay increase. Should ask for more in future.

solicitation kit for informational purposes only. When the proposal letter is to be sent out by the solicitor, the sample serves as a model outlining the case for support, which will be augmented by information found in each prospect's profile. A proposal letter incorporating information from the prospect profile on page 78 would read as follows:

Sample Proposal Letter

Dear Mr. Smith:

The XYZ Institute for 20 years has been serving our community with programs that *(list and description of programs and activities that are central to the organization's mission)* . Last year more than 20,000 people in our community directly benefited from our activities, and countless others received the indirect benefit of living in a community where efforts such as ours improve the quality of life for all.

In the past you have been an active supporter of our annual campaigns. Your gift of $1,000 last year was particularly appreciated. It helped us continue our record of 14 years without a deficit and ensured that we would be able to fund our existing programs and plan for growth. Also, your contribution of $5,000 to our endowment campaign five years ago helped get our fledgling endowment program off the ground. Today endowment provides 15% of our annual income.

Now we find ourselves in need of a new facility. We have simply outgrown our existing building. To that end, I am chairing a capital campaign to raise $1.2 million. With that money we will be able purchase the old Green's department store and turn it into a services center. I have enclosed a brochure showing architectural renderings of the new facility and listing the services it will allow us to provide.

If the past is any indication, I know we can count on your generous support in helping to make the dream of a stronger and more secure XYZ Institute come true. In order to achieve our goal of $1.2 million, friends such as you must be willing to give more generously than ever before. We hope that you will be able to make a donation in the range of $10,000.

Gary Jones will be calling you within the next week to schedule an appointment to tell you more about the plans for our new services center and to show you how your gift can help turn those plans into reality. He will also point out the ways in which we would be delighted and honored to recognize your gift.

Thank you for your past support and your willingness to give generously to make our community a better place to live through the efforts of the XYZ Institute.

Sincerely,

Bob Clarke

Campaign Chair

As you can see, the key is getting the case for support up front, including specifics showing that you value the prospect's past efforts, letting the prospect know how much he is being counted on for, and telling him who will be contacting him when to ask for it.

The proposal letter should go out on either campaign stationery or the chair's own professional stationery, whichever is more likely to impress the prospect. Campaign stationery is a useful tool for a solicitor to have, and a small supply should be included in the solicitation kit. If stationery hasn't been designed for the campaign, the organization's regular stationery can be used. Solicitors can then make the decision to use their own stationery or that of the organization when writing to prospects.

The final item in the solicitation kit is the pledge card (or envelope), which is the donor's written promise to pay. Include one for every prospect the solicitor is to contact. It is the solicitor's responsibility to pick up the pledge card and then forward it to the team captain. Sometimes the pledge card will be accompanied by payment, but space should be provided for donors to indicate a date by which they will pay.

Sample Pledge Card

```
Amount of donation  $_____    Date _____

___ Cash                                 ___ Charge card:

___ Check                                Card type _____

___ Securities                           Card no. _____

___ Payment enclosed                     Exp. date _____

___ Pledge     Date(s) to be paid _____

___ My employer will match this gift  ___ Form enclosed  ___ Form pending


Name _____
```

With a volunteer force recruited and a solicitation kit ready to be passed out, you are now ready to begin the actual campaign.

CHAPTER 14

Managing a Campaign: The What, When, and How

Once an organization has identified a financial need, agreed to raise a specific amount to help offset the need, developed a plan to reach the goal, recruited a group of volunteers to carry out the plan, and created a kit of support materials to assist the volunteers, planning and preparation are over. It's time to start managing the campaign, and the kickoff meeting is the first step in that process. Volunteers, staff members who will be involved in the campaign, and any consultants who may have been engaged need to be pulled together into a single room, informed about what is expected of them, and shown how to carry out their responsibilities.

The Kickoff Meeting

Kickoff meetings are almost always held in the late afternoon or early evening when volunteers are more likely to be free. You can serve a meal or snacks or simply offer hot and cold drinks. The formality of the affair and the amenities offered depend on what the organization can afford and what is customary in the community. (No potlucks, please.)

Depending on the size of the group, kickoff meetings can be convened in the campaign chair's home or place of business, a private room in a restaurant, or the organization's offices. The person running the meeting should be the chair of the campaign, but the program for the meeting should be set by the organization's person responsible for development.

Sample Program

1. *Executive director:* Welcome, quick description and history of the organization, and introduction of the campaign chair

2. *Campaign chair:* Thank you to volunteers; explanation of campaign objectives, goal, and structure; and introduction of person responsible for development

3. *Development person:* Pick or assign prospects

4. *Team captains:* Disseminate prospect profiles and solicitation kits

5. *Development person, with assistance of campaign chair and division chairs:* Discussion of solicitation kits and advice about how to be a successful solicitor

6. *Campaign chair:* Review campaign calendar and deadlines

7. *Campaign chair, division chairs, executive director, development person:* Answer questions

8. *Campaign chair:* Pep talk and adjournment

Once the kickoff meeting attendees have been welcomed and briefed on the goal and structure of the campaign, it is time to allocate prospects. This can be done by arbitrarily assigning them to solicitors or by letting solicitors pick their prospects from a list. I prefer the latter approach, even though it takes more time, for two reasons. It involves the solicitors in the campaign right from the start, and by picking their prospects, solicitors take on greater ownership of the campaign and the goal. However, I recommend that the list from which prospects are picked not include the suggested giving amounts. If that information is given at this time, the more timid solicitors may pick only givers with smaller potential, and the overly ambitious may try to bite off more than they can chew.

As much as I like having solicitors pick their own prospects, campaigns with large numbers of prospects and solicitors can make that process too cumbersome. When prospects are assigned, points three and four of the agenda can be combined.

After prospects have been assigned or picked and their profiles passed out, it is time to talk about the how-to of solicitation. If a strong solicitation kit has been assembled, it will function as a guide to this part of the meeting. Beginning with the case for support, each item in the kit (see Chapter 13) should be reviewed and discussed. This is also the time when more formalized, general training should be included. Role-playing demonstrations, either in person or on videotape, can be very effective here.

Experienced solicitors may need little or no training, while new solicitors may benefit from more intensive instruction offered to them and their team captains in a session immediately following the kickoff meeting. More role-playing, along with descriptions from team captains of obstacles likely to be encountered and explanations of how to overcome them, are in order here.

If new-solicitor training is to be given, it should be done the night of the kickoff meeting for two reasons. First, it is unlikely that attendance will be as high at a second general meeting. Secondly, when solicitors leave the kickoff meeting, they should be ready to start work. Having new solicitors come back for more training stalls the momentum created by the kickoff meeting.

Announcing the Campaign and Publicity

Not all campaigns will benefit from broad-scale public awareness and a major publicity effort. However, every organization has constituencies which must be made aware of each campaign undertaken. Announcing a campaign to constituency groups prepares them to be solicited.

The broader the base of prospects for a campaign, the greater the need for publicity. Annual campaigns are the most broadly based in their support; therefore, every constituency of an organization needs to be aware that one is under way. Announcement of the goal, the kickoff, major mileposts of the campaign—all become events to be publicized in the community's news media and through the organization's newsletters. The more times potential donors bump into the campaign, the better.

Because of their reliance on fewer support constituencies and fewer donors, capital and endowment campaigns benefit less from a concerted publicity effort. Publicity, under the best of circumstances, is likely to engender only a tangential awareness of a campaign. Communication to prospects of capital and endowment campaigns needs to come directly from solicitors and campaign leadership. This is the only way the intricacies of the case for support can be explained successfully to these potentially large donors. Indeed, with capital and endowment campaigns, it is best not to issue the first press release until a certain level of attainment has been reached. In effect, you announce the campaign by reporting a major gift or gifts. In capital campaigns, press releases can be issued on the progress of construction. The idea is to create a public awareness of the reason for the campaign, rather than of the campaign itself.

Bear in mind that publicity is sought only in order to support the fund-raising effort. It is possible for those managing a campaign to become too enamored with publicity and expend effort on obtaining it that would be far better spent on asking for money. Nearly every organization has a mechanism and a person or persons assigned the responsibility for publicizing activities. Campaign management should leave the planning of publicity, the issuing of press releases, and the obtaining of media coverage in the hands of this person.

Asking for the Money

The first step in asking prospects to make a donation is to send them a letter. This is true no matter the type of campaign or potential size of gift. In the small-gifts division of an annual campaign the letter may be the only step, although I would recommend having it followed up by a telephone call, if at all possible. Even in door-to-door solicitations, a letter should be sent first announcing the date of, reason for, and, in most cases, the suggested amount of the request. In the case of larger gifts, the letter announces that a solicitor will be calling for an appointment. We refer to this kind of letter as the proposal letter because it proposes that the prospect become a donor to an organization.

Proposal letters are usually signed either by the solicitor or by the campaign chair. In the case of the latter, the status and power of the chair are lent to what is essentially a request of the prospect to meet with a solicitor. If signed by the chair, you can also be sure the letters all went out by a specific time. This also forces solicitors to act by the time the letter says they will be calling for an appointment. However, not every solicitor will be able to make the initial calls in the same time frame. One or more solicitors may be out of town when the letter hits. Consequently, there is less likelihood of being in error as to when solicitors will be calling if the timing of proposal letters is left in the hands of the solicitors.

Proposal letters signed by the solicitors can be personalized to reflect the fact that solicitors and prospects have shared experiences or even know one another. It is best to make the determination of who signs and sends the proposal letters on a solicitor-by-solicitor and prospect-by-prospect basis.

This much is certain. If the letter indicates the day that someone will be knocking on the door, someone must be there on that day. If it says the prospect will be telephoned on Tuesday, the 25th, to be asked for a gift, that call must be made on the 25th. If it says the solicitor will be calling for an appointment next week, the call has to be made next week. *When asking people for money, it is vitally important to do what you say you are going to do at the time you say you are going to do it.*

In capital or endowment campaigns or when seeking larger gifts in annual campaigns, the proposal letter should be followed up with a phone call requesting an appointment. If prospects raise the question, "Is this meeting going to be about money?" solicitors should respond with a light touch, couching the request for an appointment in personal terms:

> **Don't worry, you won't need to bring your checkbook. I really would like to meet you, and I would consider it a distinct favor if you would give me the opportunity to share with you some of what is happening at the XYZ Institute.**

Never let the phone call degenerate into a request for a donation. Just as big-ticket items are seldom sold over the phone, large donations are rarely made without a face-to-face meeting.

Once an appointment has been obtained, solicitors need to show up on time, ready, willing, and able to present the case for support. Just prior to a meeting, they should review with care the donor's profile and the support materials in their solicitation kit.

The first meeting should not take place in a public space such as a restaurant with its distractions and interruptions. Solicitors should begin by talking with prospects about professional and personal interests, mutual friends and acquaintances, places and times where their lives may have crossed. However, solicitors should not forget why they are there. Quickly, but naturally, discussion of the campaign should be worked into the conversation. Solicitors should mention their own personal involvement and commitment to the organization as a way of explaining why it is of such great value to the community. They must convey how important the current fund-raising campaign is to the organization's future. When appropriate, a tour of the organization's facilities and the opportunity to meet others involved with the organization should be offered. Finally, solicitors should ask prospects to consider supporting the organization by making a pledge in the suggested amount.

Executing a fund-raising campaign means doing the same few steps over and over. Solicitors write, phone, present, ask, and report back—a process that is repeated with each prospect assigned to them. However, the process is seldom a straight line. There may be any number of phone calls to a single prospect. A solicitor might first meet with a prospect in the prospect's office and then arrange a tour of the organization or, in the case of a capital building campaign, a visit to the construction site. After that, another meeting over lunch may be required to clinch the deal. All during this process the solicitor is reporting on progress to the team captain. To be effective a solicitor must:

1. Not procrastinate in making appointments
2. Talk directly to the prospect and visit the prospect
3. Follow up with the prospect after each step
4. Never leave it up to the prospect to take the initiative
5. Follow up each solicitation with verbal or written reports to the team captain

A solicitor can be doing everything right and still run into a problem in getting appointments with prospective donors capable of making large gifts. People who can make large gifts are usually busy people. Simply getting to see them can take a few weeks. Then there is the time it takes to convince someone to part with thousands, tens of thousands, hundreds of thousands, or even millions of dollars. The larger the sum of money involved, the less likely that a 30-minute appointment on a Wednesday morning will do the job. Solicitors must be prepared to put in whatever time and effort will be required to get a final answer, and they have to be careful not to pressure a prospect into a no. Soliciting is exactly like selling. Prospects have to be made comfortable, shown the value of a contribution, and encouraged to make positive decisions. They have to be flattered, cajoled, appealed to, convinced, and ultimately sold.

Sooner or later a solicitor will get a final answer from a prospect. It will take one of four forms. The prospect will say:

1. Yes, to the suggested amount
2. Yes, to a lesser amount
3. No, not at this time
4. No, don't ever contact me again

Obviously the first response is best, and the second, depending on how much less, isn't too bad either. When you get one of those two answers, you say thank you, take the money or the pledge card, and leave. That day or, at the latest, the next, you report the gift to your team captain and send a thank-you note to the donor.

If the gift is less than hoped for, even if it is substantially less, never show disappointment. Don't say, "But we were hoping for more." Don't frown. Don't roll your eyes. Don't even ask why it is less. Ninety-nine times out of a hundred, the donor has already told you why. To ask now embarrasses you by showing you weren't paying attention and embarrasses the donor by forcing him or her to go back over the reasons why he or she was unwilling or unable to give at the suggested level.

When the answer is no, not at this time, it is still necessary to thank the person for considering your request. You should try to find out if perhaps later in the campaign the situation could be more favorable. If you are told it might be, you put that in your report and encourage the organization to follow up at the appropriate time. If there is no chance of a gift for the current campaign, give up. Don't poison the well. Graciously accept the no, and leave the prospect for the next campaign and the next solicitor. After all, it might be you.

When the answer is no, don't ever contact me again, you need to leave with an understanding of the reasons why the response was so adamantly negative. If you have been listening, you probably already know. If you are getting this response over the phone, ask why the prospect wants to be dropped from the organization's list. Take this information back to the organization and let the person responsible for development deal with it.

When I was conducting telefunding campaigns as development director of the Cleveland Orchestra, I would look at the reports on persons who the night before had asked to be taken off our list. Some of them would be people who had given us $250 or $500 or even $1,000 in the past. I would call them and say, "I know you said no, and we will take you off our list, but I want to be sure we are taking you off because of something that we can't fix or is out of our control." They would, invariably, appreciate the call and would tell me if they indeed wanted to be taken off the list because of a grievance. Sometimes the reason was something we could fix. Sometimes they would even reconsider and make a gift, but I never asked them to. The purpose of my call was to save these prospects for the future, if possible, and to find out if we had done something wrong.

Once a prospect tells a solicitor no, you have to honor that answer. To do otherwise, to try to pressure, shame, or intimidate a prospect who has clearly said no, is to compromise your organization. Such tactics rarely will bring in any money and nearly always create bad feelings.

Progress: Reports, Meetings, and Sharing the Information

How do you keep a fund-raising campaign on track? By being well organized, constantly monitoring progress, and informing all campaign participants of that progress. The very reason for the pyramidal structure of a campaign committee is to simplify management. In the best of circumstances, the pyramid is constructed so that no person supervises more than five people. (To maintain this limit is why we sometimes add campaign and divisional co-chairs.) Managing even the largest campaigns then becomes a matter of monitoring the progress of a limited number of small hierarchical units. Team captains track the efforts of solicitors, divisional chairs make sure that captains are on top of their teams, and the campaign chair keeps tabs on the divisions. However, this system works only if information moves upward quickly. You can't fix a problem in a campaign unless you know there is a problem.

The best way to make sure that information is being shared is to schedule monthly progress meetings. Attendees know they will be expected to report on their area of responsibility—what has been done, who has been contacted, how much money has been raised. The monthly progress meeting gives the campaign leaders a deadline by which they need to have their houses in order.

It is unlikely that you would reconvene at these progress meetings everyone who attended the kickoff meeting. The logistics are just too cumbersome. Unless the campaign leadership is an especially large group, the ideal progress meeting consists of the campaign chair, divisional chairs, team captains, the organization's development person, and the development consultant, if one is being used. In really large campaigns or in ones where some divisions have a great many teams, it may be better to have the division chairs meet independently with their team captains rather than include so many participants in an overall meeting.

A couple of days before a meeting, team captains should submit written progress reports to the division chairs. Then the day before a meeting, the division chairs consolidate those reports and turn them over to the campaign chair.

CAMPAIGN TRACKING REPORT

	A	B	C	D	E	F	
Campaign Reporting Division	Goal of the Campaign	Booked Gifts from Previous Donors to Date	Booked Gifts from New Donors to Date	Estimated Gifts from Previous Donors Yet to Be Reported	Estimated Gifts from New Donors Yet to Be Reported	Projected Amount to Be Realized B+C+D+E	Projected Difference from Goal A – F
Individuals	$____	$____	$____	$____	$____	$____	$____
$1,000 and over	$____	$____	$____	$____	$____	$____	$____
Under $1,000	$____	$____	$____	$____	$____	$____	$____
Corporations	$____	$____	$____	$____	$____	$____	$____
Large	$____	$____	$____	$____	$____	$____	$____
Small	$____	$____	$____	$____	$____	$____	$____
Foundations	$____	$____	$____	$____	$____	$____	$____
Trustees	$____	$____	$____	$____	$____	$____	$____
TOTALS	$____	$____	$____	$____	$____	$____	$____

The first item on the agenda of a progress meeting is an update from the campaign chair based on the reports he has received from the division chairs. This update details how much money has been raised and reports on major gifts. Next follows an assessment of the campaign's progress—the real business of the meeting. How does the money raised stack up against what was expected from the donors? How many donors have given less than their rated level—and how much less? Which past donors expected to give to this campaign have been lost altogether? After adding the dollars raised so far to the amount projected to be received from the remaining prospects, how much money will the campaign raise? Will the goal be achieved? A written report of the foregoing should be passed out to all following the meeting.

The campaign chair's written report on overall and divisional progress should also be sent to campaign participants who did not attend a progress meeting, including solicitors. I find that a campaign newsletter is the best vehicle for distributing information for the duration of the campaign. At the very least, the newsletter should be published shortly after each progress meeting. Special editions are a great way to announce major gifts and events. A campaign newsletter is not the *New York Times*. Keep it simple, on a timely basis. A single sheet printed on two sides is fine. If you have more news, add more pages. Be sure to get the newsletter into the volunteers' hands. They need to know that campaign management is on top of things and that progress is being made.

There are two things that you do not want to do at a progress meeting. Do not create a competitive atmosphere among divisions and among teams within a division. The campaign succeeds when every division, team, and solicitor succeeds. People should be invested in the campaign, not in their particular team or division. You should also avoid calling attention publicly to a person's failure to perform. Remember, these are volunteers. Just as we would not shame a prospective donor for failing to meet our expectations, we should not humiliate a volunteer whose efforts have fallen short.

You want volunteers leaving a progress meeting with a clear understanding of where the campaign stands and a renewed commitment to get the job done. If the campaign is on track, getting that commitment isn't hard. But if the money booked to date added to the unreported gifts total ends up somewhere south of the goal, then it's time for reassessment and adjustment.

Mid-Course Corrections and Problem Solving

We track progress in a fund-raising campaign in order to identify problems in time to take corrective actions so that the goal stays within reach. If at any point in the campaign it begins to look as if the ability to achieve the goal is slipping away, then those managing the campaign must stop and take stock of the situation.

The most common problem encountered during a campaign is the failure of solicitors to gain commitments from the proven base of donors for the amounts which the rating and evaluating process ascribed to them.

Early tracking of progress is crucial. It is better to find out that results are 15 percent below estimate after 10 percent of the prospects have made their donations than after half have been solicited. Once a campaign is under way, the steps you can take to make up a projected shortfall are limited, but the earlier you do them, the greater the effect they will have.

What can you do to cover a projected shortfall and get a campaign back on track?

1. Ask trustees and campaign leadership to increase their gifts
2. Increase the suggested giving for prospects yet to be solicited
3. Identify additional prospects to be solicited
4. Go back to selected donors who have already given and ask them to increase their gifts

If it looks as if the goal is not going to be reached, go to the campaign's strongest constituency—the organization's trustees and the campaign's volunteer leaders. They have a special interest in the campaign's success, and will be making gifts, probably substantial gifts, to the campaign anyway. Ask them to up the ante.

Next, rework your ratings and evaluations for prospects yet to be solicited. Either increase the suggested gift level for all by a set percentage, or, better yet, go back and reassess them individually to a higher level. If proposal letters have been sent out with a suggested giving level, that's water over the dam. Go ahead and make the change anyway. The solicitors can explain the need for a larger gift during their presentations. In fact, this "problem" can give added impetus to their solicitations. They can take the negative of a projected shortfall and turn it into a positive argument for increased support.

The third thing you can do to offset a projected shortfall is to broaden the base of the campaign by finding new prospects using the prospecting techniques discussed in Chapter 6. With the exception of some direct-mail campaigns, an organization rarely contacts a majority of the persons capable of giving to it. Once again, the negative of a shortfall can be turned into a positive. New prospects will be contacted and the proven donor base will be enlarged for future campaigns.

As a final recourse, comb the list of those who have already given to the campaign. Who among them has proved to be a special friend of the organization in the past? It is to those carefully selected persons that you should return with a request that they increase their gifts. The fact they have already given shows that they bought into the case for support of the campaign. Go back to them, and go over the case again, calmly explaining why it is necessary that they give more and how *they* are the ones who are needed to make the campaign a success. Sure, it's embarrassing to have to go back to them, but not half as embarrassing as having to explain to them and other constituencies that you failed to raise the money needed. I've had to do both, and I would rather ask an organization's supporters to increase their gifts than face them with a campaign that failed to achieve its goal.

A discrepancy between donor ratings and actual gifts received isn't the only problem that can beset a campaign. Solicitors will typically complain that they are having trouble reaching their prospects—they're out of town or just too busy to meet with them. That may be true, at least in some instances, but usually the "problem" is with solicitors, who need to put more effort into their follow-through. Sometimes they will have slacked off a little because they don't want to keep bugging someone. (Of course, a prospect who simply will not take a solicitor's calls has to be written off for that campaign.) Sometimes solicitors find themselves under increased work pressure—their company is merging, the workforce is being downsized, they have a new boss. Sometimes the pressure comes from home—a new baby, buying a house, marital problems, a death in the family. And sometimes solicitors just don't do what they have promised. When a solicitor, for whatever reason, is not bringing back answers from prospects, it is up to the team captain to solve the problem. In the end, it may be necessary for the captain to take responsibility for calling on some or all of the solicitor's prospects.

Another omnipresent complaint from those working the frontlines is that there isn't enough publicity. You can have generated reams of publicity, and they will still feel it isn't enough. This is a phantom complaint. Publicity just isn't that important in most campaigns. It comes from solicitors and team captains who are not making progress. You won't hear it from those who actually have something to report.

Then there is negative publicity—everything from an officer of the organization being indicted for stealing to employees out on strike. United Way knows about the former problem, and I encountered the latter once when the Cleveland Orchestra's musicians took to the picket lines. When something terrible happens, invariably there are people who want to stop the campaign. "Put it on hold!" is their cry. "Wait until this blows over, then restart the campaign," they say.

Never, ever stop a campaign because of negative publicity. A campaign deferred is a campaign defeated. Volunteers will disappear. Previous donors not yet solicited will be less likely to give when the campaign is restarted. People who have already given money will be left wondering what is going to happen to their gift. Pledges will be rescinded. No matter what the negative publicity is, halting a fund-raising campaign will make it worse. The media will hop on the suspended campaign as an indication that the organization is in even deeper trouble.

The other major problems I have had come up in a campaign all involve the loss of key players. Once my entire development staff—the people recording gifts, sending out acknowledgments, and doing many other things—was wiped out by flu for nearly two weeks. Those of us who remained on our feet just worked harder, and when the others came back we played catch-up. Solicitors, team captains, division chairs, even the campaign chair can all disappear during a campaign. People quit, change jobs, and even die. Twice the chairs of large campaigns on which I was working left town during their campaigns. Once we recovered nicely. The other time the campaign flagged.

Replacing solicitors is a smallish problem. Replacing team captains is a little bigger quandary, and finding new division chairs is a real headache. But a campaign that loses its chair teeters on the brink of disaster. Obviously you look for team captains to replace lost solicitors or take on the work themselves. Division chairs should be able to replace a team captain, and the campaign chair, with some assistance, can either personally handle the work of a division chair or find a stand-in. But replacing a campaign chair in the middle of a campaign is a real job, and it's the job of an organization's trustees. Ideally the president of the board or an influential trustee is both right for the job and ready to take it on. Barring that, perhaps a division chair could be persuaded to step up. Maybe there is somebody within the departing chair's company who can fill the bill, or perhaps the organization's board president will call in a big favor. Just as recruiting a campaign chair is the job of trustees, so is finding a replacement for one.

Tracking Gifts and Collecting the Money

Receiving and recording gifts is simple to do, but very often poorly done. When donors make a gift or a pledge, solicitors notify their team captain and forward the pledge card or check to the organization's development office that day. If the deal is struck in the evening, they do it first thing the next morning. The timing and process is where the first mistakes are made. The timing is do it immediately. The process is send the paperwork to the development office. There is no need for checks and pledge cards to go anyplace other than to the organization. These are official documents and should be collected in one central location as soon as they are signed. No solicitor should ever hold a check or pledge card while waiting for others to come in. Stamps and envelopes are inexpensive. Bad will created by a lost or slowly processed check or pledge card can be very costly.

Once the paperwork reaches the organization, checks and pledges should be recorded, checks deposited, and acknowledgments sent to donors that day, or at the very latest the next. Held checks too easily become misplaced checks. You want to avoid having any donor call to tell you the check hasn't shown up in their bank statement and have them wondering whether you received it. Quick acknowledgment shows that the gift is appreciated and the organization efficient. That acknowledgment need be nothing more than a preprinted card or a form letter from the chair of the campaign. However, in this age of the computer, what could be easier than a personalized form letter from the campaign chair on his business letterhead, that of the organization, or special campaign stationery?

Sample Acknowledgment Letter

Dear _____:

   (Solicitor)   has forwarded your check for $_____ to our campaign headquarters. I want to let you know how deeply we appreciate your generous gift. The money we are raising during this campaign will allow the XYZ Institute to refurbish its facilities and offer help to more people in our community than ever before. Again, thank you for your generosity and leadership. With your help we are building a better community.

Sincerely,
Bob Clarke
Campaign Chair

Whatever format you choose, the important thing is to get the acknowledgment out when you receive the check or pledge. Don't wait!

When a pledge is received, the question becomes how and when to collect the pledge. If the donor has indicated when he will be sending payment, reiterate that information in the acknowledgment letter (pertinent addition and changes are in italics):

> Dear _____:
>
> __(Solicitor)__ has forwarded your *pledge* for $_____ to our campaign headquarters. I want to let you know how deeply we appreciate your generous gift. The money we are raising during this campaign will allow the XYZ Institute to refurbish its facilities and offer help to more people in our community than ever before.
>
> *From your pledge card it is our understanding that you will be making payment by* __(date)__ . Again, thank you for your generosity and leadership. With your help we are building a better community.
>
> Sincerely,
Bob Clarke
Campaign Chair

If a donor makes no indication of when he will be fulfilling a pledge, don't go back and ask. Arbitrarily assign a date two or three months in the future as indicated in the acknowledgment letter (pertinent additions and changes are in italics):

> Dear _____:
>
> __(Solicitor)__ has forwarded your pledge for $_____ to our campaign headquarters. I want to let you know how deeply we appreciate your generous gift. The money we are raising during this campaign will allow the XYZ Institute to refurbish its facilities and offer help to more people in our community than ever before.
>
> *In order to close our books on the campaign in a timely fashion, we will send you a statement reflecting your pledge and asking for it to be remitted to us in* __(month)__ *if we have not already received your donation by that time.* Again, thank you for your generosity and leadership. With your help we are building a better community.
>
> Sincerely,
Bob Clarke
Campaign Chair

The acknowledgment letter brings closure to the solicitation process. It records the outcome of the solicitation, and it announces any follow-up yet to come on the part of the organization. A copy of the acknowledgment letter should be forwarded to the appropriate solicitor and team captain to let them know that the organization can account for the paperwork and checks.

Announcing Results and Saying Thank You

The campaign's over and the goal has been achieved. Life is good.

Issue a press release and a final newsletter thanking campaign leadership, volunteer solicitors, and the donors. Single out people who should be commended, and praise the campaign chair. I like to host a thank-you function or functions for my volunteers. The format should be in tune with the organization and the community—a cocktail party, picnic, or open house, for example. (Don't forget to seek underwriting for this event.) If appropriate, have a function for large donors.

The campaign's over and the goal has not been achieved. Life has been better.

This has happened to me more times than I like to admit. Goals and resources do not always match, campaigns do develop insurmountable problems, and sometimes you just can't pull it off. Fund-raisers have to be prepared for the occasional failure. However, bear in mind that a campaign can come up short of its goal and still have demonstrated a lot of accomplishment. You may still be able to say congratulations to volunteers and donors. The money raised may be an all-time high for the organization's annual fund. More donors than ever before may have given. The campaign may have come within 10 percent of a goal we knew to be very ambitious. It is the rare campaign in which you cannot find a positive accomplishment to call to the attention of volunteers, donors, and the public.

So issue a press release and a final newsletter thanking campaign leadership, volunteer solicitors, and the donors. Single out people who should be commended, and praise the campaign chair. Thank-you functions are still appropriate. Donors still need to be told how much they are valued and appreciated. With the people who worked on the campaign, you need to be practical and honest about the disappointment, but don't let words of regret, frustration, and unhappiness get to the ears of those who gave. If you become preoccupied with the shortfall and forget about all the good things that happened, you do a disservice to those who worked a campaign and to those who gave to it. They should never be left to think their efforts or gifts were a waste.

The Key to Running a Good Campaign

In a word, organization. If all pre-kickoff activities were well conceived and executed, then the campaign in all likelihood will succeed, *if its management and implementation are well organized.* Good organization gives a campaign the means to maneuver around the tough spots and work through problems. It allows the campaign leadership to deal with the process of raising money rather than the process of managing a fund-raising campaign.

Good organization maximizes resources. Disorganization stretches resources to their breaking point. Good organization communicates and instills confidence in volunteers. Disorganization leaves workers out on a limb and gives them an excuse for not following through. Good organization is invisible to donors. Disorganization is the first thing they see. Good organization ensures that a campaign runs according to plan. Disorganization makes the time seem too short and the goal too high. Win or lose, good organization leaves a reward of knowledge. Win or lose, disorganization leaves a residue of confusion.

CHAPTER 15

Assessment and Review: What Was Accomplished and What Was Learned

It's over. The campaign is finished. The thank-you's have been said and the money counted. However, before closing the book on a campaign for good, you should take one last look at it. The days immediately following a campaign are the time to analyze what went wrong and what went right, which fixes worked and which didn't.

You should assess and review every fund-raising campaign, and you should make a record of what you find. Evaluation is the final procedure in a well-organized fund-raising campaign, and the report you write based on that evaluation is the organized record of the knowledge you acquired. File that report and it will be a database for you to draw on. Hindsight is 20/20. Turn it into foresight for the next campaign.

All the participants in a campaign should be asked to evaluate their area of responsibility and the volunteers with whom they worked. You want to determine what the campaign did well and not so well, which expectations were realistic and which weren't, which tools worked and which didn't, and who performed well and who didn't. Solicitors, team captains, division chairs, and campaign chairs should each make their own evaluation, but no evaluation is more important than that of the staff members charged with designing, organizing, and running campaigns. They, after all, are the ones who are going to have to manage the next campaign, so it is from their perspective that we will look at the evaluation process.

The first rule in evaluating a campaign is *don't wait*. The farther away you get from a campaign, the less you and others will remember, and every day you delay your evaluation is a brick in the wall of inertia you must climb to start the process. Begin your evaluation the day after the close of the campaign.

Let's start with the things you want to learn. What is it you wish to know about a campaign that can help with the next one?

1. Was the goal realistic?
2. How well did the organizational structure of the campaign work?
3. Did the solicitation kit materials do the expected job?
4. Was the kickoff meeting effective?
5. Were the progress meetings and reports to volunteers effective?
6. Was the campaign able to fix problems and replace volunteers quickly and effectively?
7. Did the development office function adequately?
8. Which volunteers performed well, and who fell down?

The answers to those eight questions can be synthesized from an analysis of information from five different sources:

1. Your own record and recollection of campaign events and occurrences
2. Other campaign workers' recollections
3. Notes of progress meetings and progress reports
4. The quantifiable results—who gave how much
5. Prospects' and donors' experiences

At first blush, the question of whether the goal was realistic seems to be self-evident. If it was achieved, it was. If it was missed by a lot, it wasn't. However, like most things in life, the issue is not that simple. A goal easily achieved could have been an unrealistically low goal or the result of a totally unexpected large gift, while a failure to meet a goal could have been due to a poorly designed or executed campaign, rather than the goal having been set too high. Whether or not the goal was realistic is a question that may have to await the answers to the other seven questions.

In assessing how well prospects were rated and evaluated, you need to determine if there was a consistency of results. Did the vast majority of donors give substantially under their rated level? Did a large number of previous donors reduce their gifts or decline to contribute altogether? Was the ratio of new donors to new prospects contacted in line with that of previous campaigns? This information is easily obtained from an analysis of gifts and pledges.

The best way to determine the effectiveness of the organizational structure of the campaign is to look at the campaign's interim progress reports and to interview those who took part in it. What we are searching for here is not isolated instances of persons failing to perform their jobs, but a pattern of underperformance. Was there a division where a number of team captains came up short? If so, the division chair may have been spread too thin, and a division co-chair may have been needed. Do the progress reports show a pattern of solicitors having a hard time following up with their calls? If so, there may have been too many prospects assigned to each solicitor. Look at how the pyramid of campaign management was structured and determine whether that structure had weak points. If the weak points were many and spread throughout a single level of the structure or if they were grouped vertically within one part of the pyramid, then it is likely that there was a problem in structure. If the weak points are random, and no pattern can be identified, then it is likely that they are a result of poor individual performance.

To find out how well the tools in the solicitation kit worked, ask the solicitors. Query them individually either by phone or in a questionnaire, or convene a focus group or groups. If you go the route of a focus group, make sure that you keep the group on topic. Don't let them rehash the entire campaign. Focus their attention, and they will provide a better, more detailed analysis. Also, be sure to draw your participants from a number of teams.

Analysis of how the kickoff meeting went is best done right after the event. Your evaluation of it should be based largely on a review of your notes and the comments you collected from participants at the time. To this you can add new information, such as problems that occurred during the campaign with material that was covered during the kickoff meeting.

Progress meetings and progress reports are the maintenance procedures of a fund-raising campaign. If they uncovered problems and helped you to track the progress of the campaign, they did their job. Did you do yours? Did you hold all scheduled progress meetings? Was attendance good? Did you issue reports and the campaign newsletter immediately following each meeting? Did you respond immediately to problems identified at the meetings?

What you do to fix the problems progress meetings uncover can make or break a campaign. In order to fix a problem, you have to be prepared to act as soon as it is identified. Go back to your progress reports and see how long it took you to solve problems. Were you able to replace a missing volunteer, add new prospects to the list, get slow-acting solicitors moving, limit the damage of negative publicity, and handle any of the myriad other things that can go wrong in a campaign quickly and effectively? If the problem came back in the next meeting or if results slipped as a result of it, the answer is no. If that is the case, ask yourself what went wrong and how you could have dealt with the problem differently.

Evaluating the development office is a relatively straightforward process. Were gifts booked, calls made, and acknowledgments sent accurately and according to schedule? If not, you may need to change procedures or personnel before the next campaign.

Until this point, you have been looking for breakdowns in the organizational structure or procedures of the campaign. Now you look for persons who failed. This is the most delicate and often the most important part of your post-campaign assessment.

Campaigns live and die by the quality of volunteers who work them. People who don't do the job need to be weeded out. The last thing you want is a division chair, who fell down, becoming next year's annual campaign chair.

Actually identifying the persons who failed is the easiest part of the entire evaluation process. First you look at the results. Did the solicitors, team captains, division chairs, and campaign chair deliver as expected? Ask the campaign chair how the division chairs performed, the division chairs how the team captains worked out, and the team captains how well their solicitors performed.

Once you have gathered all the above information and analyzed it, you are ready to write your report. For your own file make it no-holds-barred. Evaluate everything and everyone ruthlessly, but with no personal bias, and do it very confidentially. However, you will need to share the results of the assessment with the campaign chair, the board's standing development committee, and the chair of the board of trustees. For these audiences you need to write a report that accurately documents how the campaign progressed, but does not point a finger at particular persons. Present the evidence, and indicate what actions were taken to solve problems. Let the readers draw their own conclusions.

If the first rule in evaluating a campaign is don't wait, the second is *get the evaluation done quickly.* You should be finished within a week of the campaign's close. It's time to move on to other things.

CHAPTER 16

Developing the Development Team

The *givers* who provide the money, the *getters* who ask for the money, and the *facilitators* who make the asking and giving possible are the three columns upon which a successful fund-raising program rests. Take away any one of them, and an organization's funding base collapses. Weaken one, and an organization's financial balance becomes precarious. In Chapters 5 and 6, we looked at the givers, examining who they are and why they give. In this concluding chapter, we will look at the getters and facilitators, exploring their essential characteristics and how they need to work together.

A successful development operation is the result of many people working together for a common goal. It is a team effort. A development team is comprised of an organization's getters and facilitators. The getters are the volunteers who sit on committees and work fund-raising campaigns. The facilitators are the organization's development staff, consultants, and other staff members. The members of any team bring a diverse mesh of experience, ability, temperament, and expectation to the table, and each functional role on a development team is best fulfilled by persons exhibiting certain configurations of those four qualities.

The Development Director and Staff

While not all non-profit organizations have professional fund-raising officers on staff, any organization that counts on contributed income to provide a substantial portion of its budget *should* have a professional development director. In small organizations, the development director could conceivably be a volunteer. However, the important thing is that within even the smallest of non-profits, someone is given as his or her primary organization responsibility the coordination and implementation of contributed income programs. A development director's principal charge is to create numerous, efficient, and compelling opportunities for donors to support an organization and to make the experience of giving satisfying and rewarding.

It is not a good idea for an organization's executive director to also fill the role of development director. If the organization has a valid mission, the executive director has a full-time role to play in coordinating and carrying out that mission. Fund-raising needs to be someone's primary concern. To illustrate that point, look at the following breakdown of the time spent by a generic development director on various important activities:

1. Plan fund-raising campaigns and activities   25%
2. Manage fund-raising campaigns and activities   25%
3. Recruit and train volunteer fund-raising leadership   15%
4. Identify and cultivate prospective donors   10%
5. Stay on top of advancements and changes that are pertinent to raising money within the community, to the organization's mission and programs, and to the development profession   10%
6. Forecast and evaluate the potential of fund-raising campaigns and activities   5%
7. Produce solicitation materials and train volunteer solicitors for fund-raising campaigns   5%
8. Manage personnel within the development department and interact with other organization staff members   5%

Does this look like a job that can be done well as an adjunct to another? Even more telling is the mix of qualities that make for a successful development director.

Two of the best development professionals I know are Joyce Braun and Ellen Feuer. They worked with me for several years at the Cleveland Orchestra and now run their own development departments at major institutions. Over the years, many people came to us looking for work in development and asking for job-hunting advice. After an interview we would often discuss our visitor's "qualities" as a potential development professional. Eventually we made a game out of appraising the development potential of people we came across in situations where we could observe them in action. The best opportunities to play this game turned out to be at meetings that either were held in restaurants or were catered. Depending on the attitudes our often harried and hurried servers would display and the responses they would make to our complaints, we would give a thumbs up or down as to whether we would hire them for a junior position in the Orchestra's development department.

Would you hire someone for development work like the server who replied when told that a steak was cold, "But it can't be," or "I don't know what's wrong with that chef back there"? Wouldn't you rather hire someone with the sensitivity to respond, "I'm very sorry, sir. Please let me take it back and bring you your steak the way you want it"? Determining whether a person's temperament is suited to development work is almost that simple. I hire and recommend entry-level development people largely based on their temperament and affability. How well they deal with criticism, are likely to handle volunteers and donors who are disappointed or upset, and show gratitude are key indicators.

Development professionals must have a temperament suited to serving people's needs. They have to be attentive, persistent, and flexible. They need to have a thick skin, and to be willing to hide their light under a bushel. In fund-raising, the glory goes to the getters, not the facilitators. Part of the development director's job is to make the volunteers look good, even at his or her own expense.

Development professionals need to exhibit a demeanor that is a little self-effacing. While the trustees, donors, and volunteers with whom we deal may regard us as accomplished professionals, they nevertheless appreciate a touch of deference when we are seeking their help and money. It's not that they want us to be subservient, but there is an almost imperceptible level just slightly below that of peer where they are most comfortable placing us. Many, many times I have addressed benefactors younger than I as Mr., Mrs., Ms., or Miss. Often I have had relationships of some years' duration without it ever being suggested that I call them by their first names.

Knowing your place as a development officer is a practice which I believe made me more effective during my years at the Cleveland Orchestra. Let me illustrate. Whenever I chanced upon important female contributors in the lobby prior to concerts and during intermissions, I would extend my hand and lock my arm to receive their handshake, avoiding the obligatory buss on the cheek they reserved for friends and social acquaintances. I did not want major donors to see me as one of them on a social level. What I wanted was to be one of them in the context of support for the Orchestra we all loved. At all times, I worked to keep my relationships with donors on a professional, not a social, level. As a result, my donor acquaintances felt comfortable calling me with requests for assistance and special treatment. Had they seen me as someone they needed to treat as a social equal, it is unlikely I would have been asked for help in that way. My willingness to provide deferential assistance, in the name of the Cleveland Orchestra, indebted them to it and disposed them toward making ever larger gifts.

A development director must be capable of functioning in a support role and deriving professional satisfaction from working in the background. As development director of the Cleveland Orchestra, I was not its artistic director, nor was I a musician. The work I did behind the scenes made it possible for others to make the music and be in the spotlight. I found that personally and professionally satisfying. No matter the organization, development professionals make an indirect, not a direct, contribution to its accomplishments. When they do their jobs well, they function in the background without calling attention to themselves. Just as public acclaim for fund-raising achievement is reserved for the volunteers, the glory of an organization's accomplishments belongs to those who have direct responsibility for fulfilling its mission.

The skills of a good development director are much the same as those of a good sales manager. It is the job of an organization's development director to inspire his salespersons—the volunteer solicitors—and arm them with all the tools they need to be successful. At the same time development directors must be able to run a tight ship and bring a sense of control, perspective, and order to the process of raising money.

Good development directors are donor-driven rather than institution-driven. They function as the donors' voice within the organization, bringing donor cares and concerns to staff and trustees. Yet they must remain conscious and protective of the integrity and purpose of the organization. They are in the best position to say no to a request which asks too much of the organization and undermines its mission.

The number of cultural, health, religious, social service, and educational organizations that must conduct fund-raising campaigns has increased dramatically in the past decade. Well-trained and experienced development officers are in high demand. A perusal of the Sunday want ads in any big-city newspaper turns up a surprising number of positions for experienced development directors, and national non-profit trade journals such as the *Chronicle of Philanthropy* are packed with such advertisements. Yet good development officers are hard to find. One reason for this may be that there is no proven training ground for development officers other than the process of apprenticeship in such mid-level and junior positions as associate and assistant director; director of annual, endowment, or capital giving; and development associate (which is often largely an administrative-assistant job). However, except for colleges and universities, only a relative handful of really large non-profit organizations budget for more than a single professional development position, with the result that only a shallow pool of development professionals have had the opportunity to grow incrementally in experience and responsibility.

It is unfortunate that more organizations do not see the parallels between the role of development director in the non-profit community and that of sales manager in the business world. Corporate downsizing has put on the streets many mature, capable persons experienced in sales and customer-service management who could function well as development personnel. Both sales managers and development directors need superior organizational and communication skills, a service orientation, analytic capabilities, and conceptual skills. What the former sales manager lacks in knowledge of fund-raising-specific management can be learned from seminars and books such as this one.

Instead, organizations often turn to persons with public relations or promotion experience within a non-profit setting and try to convert them into development professionals. Almost invariably, this approach is a mistake. PR persons are usually idea generators who are great at creating a favorable climate for an organization. Where they fall down is in the day-to-day care and feeding of a campaign: the slogging process of building a network of volunteers, training them, and so on. The temperament and expectations of PR professionals and development professionals are different enough that it is almost impossible someone could star in both disciplines.

If I were hiring a person to run a development operation and had to pick someone with no previous professional fund-raising experience, I would look for someone such as the head of a department within a retail operation like a department store. This person would have managed a sales staff, worked at making products available to customers, handled customer concerns and complaints, conducted special sales programs, and attended to the minutiae of day-to-day operations. Exactly what a development director does.

Consultants

Fund-raising consultants can be a godsend to non-profits. For organizations with an inexperienced, small, or nonexistent development staff, they can do everything from mentoring a budding development director to designing specific campaigns and tools to setting up the organizational structure for an ongoing fund-raising effort. Larger organizations with considerable experience in fund-raising and a fully professional development staff can benefit from a consultant's mastery of the process of initiating new types of fund-raising efforts and reorienting the development department.

Basically there are two types of consultants:

1. National or regional firms offering a full range of services and a large staff experienced in all facets of fund-raising and well versed in the needs of all types of non-profit organizations

2. Locally based individual consultants or minimally staffed firms that know a particular community's fund-raising climate and resources and perhaps specialize in one or more broad types of non-profit organizations—the arts, education, health care, social services, etc.

Generally, the first category of consultants will work only with organizations that have an established history of service and a successful fund-raising record. They are akin to investment brokers who will handle an individual's account only if he has $100,000 on deposit. While their attitude may seem discriminatory and elitist, major consulting firms do not want to be confronted with organizational and board leadership problems, insufficient staff and volunteers, an indistinct mission, or any of the other likely deterrents to conducting a successful fund-raising effort. They exist to bring more know-how to an organization which is already well grounded and has the financial base to afford the not inconsiderable cost of their services. Such firms charge in the neighborhood of $1,250 a day plus expenses and are likely to require contracts of some length.

For non-profits that are smaller, less well defined, new, or relatively inexperienced at fund-raising, consultants from the second grouping are likely to be able to do more and at a lower cost. Often, they are individuals who have a successful track record as development director at one or more organizations within the community. They know the lay of the land—who has given how much to what causes and who has the ability to lead a campaign. Local fund-raising consultants can mentor an organization's board and fledgling development staff. They are more likely to be able to help with any institutional problems hamstringing an organization's fund-raising efforts. They probably have dealt with similar obstacles in the past while facing the same resource constraints. They are likely to be more willing and able to help an organization develop a workable strategic plan, write a clearer mission statement, enlarge its volunteer base, or undertake a maiden fund-raising effort. Their intimate knowledge of a community's donor and volunteer base can make them invaluable. Many individual consultants and small firms will charge by the hour, and their daily rates are likely to be in the neighborhood of $500.

A proposal from a first-class consulting firm, large or small, to act as counsel in a fund-raising campaign would likely include the offer to help determine:

1. The case for support
2. The campaign plan
3. Key prospects and their suggested giving levels
4. Individual strategies for major-gift solicitations
5. Volunteer leadership
6. Volunteer solicitors
7. The proportion of gifts to be sought from corporations, foundations, and individuals
8. The campaign goal

Consultants expect to be made familiar with an organization's financial projections and strategic planning process, and to be involved in the articulation of its mission (at least in terms of how it will be presented during the campaign). Consultants need to meet and work with key staff members and trustees of the organization. The extent to which an organization must rely on consulting services for a campaign depends, to a great degree, on how much of the planning and execution of the campaign can be done by the development department. The less able the development department is to handle the planning and management of a campaign, the greater will be the organization's need and outlay for consulting services.

Consultants should not be thought of as a replacement for either the staff or the volunteer leadership of a campaign; they are an addition to the campaign team, hired so that an organization can move more quickly and aggressively because of their added professional experience and judgment.

The best way to choose a consultant is to ask other non-profits in the community for recommendations and then interview those candidates who look as if they might fill the bill. Request a written proposal that includes a firm estimate of time and charges. Always be sure to talk with both a principal of the consulting organization and the person who will be handling the assignment day to day, and include a cancellation clause in the contract that requires no more than 30-days' notice.

There are four absolute caveats in engaging consultants:

1. Never hire consultants whose regimen and methodology are unyielding. Consultants should be flexible in the services they provide and willing to adapt to an organization's processes.
2. Never hire consultants who request that they be paid a percentage of the funds raised in a campaign. This is regarded as unethical by the industry.
3. Never hire consultants unless you are committed to taking their advice and following their counsel. To do otherwise is to throw your money away.
4. Never hire consultants to ask for the money. That's the job of your volunteers.

Volunteers

Volunteers are the lifeblood of a development operation, and trustees are the most important volunteers of all. The trustees approve an organization's budget and they must accept personal responsibility for raising called-for contributed income. They are expected to set the pace in giving, recruiting other volunteers, and soliciting major donors. It is the rare board of trustees that is made up of persons who all can give at equally high levels. However, each trustee must be prepared to give generously at the level which he or she can support.

Too often I have been engaged as a consultant only to have the executive director of the organization or chair of the board of trustees tell me, "Our board doesn't raise money, and most of them are not in a position to make significant contributions themselves. You'll have to look elsewhere for fund-raising leadership." That's when I tell them they have to change the makeup of the board. A board must include individuals capable of making significant contributions to the organization and leading a major fund-raising campaign. Before being asked to serve as a trustee a person should be rated and evaluated for giving potential. In general, trustees' gifts should total at least 20 percent of the annual funds raised.

Obviously the most important trustee in the eyes of the development director is the chair of the board. The chair sets the tone for the organization and its volunteers. Other trustees look to the chair for leadership, and the chair has primary responsibility for volunteer leadership recruitment. However, a development director may have an even more meaningful relationship, on a day-to-day basis, with the chair of the board's standing committee for development, in that they collaborate on the planning and execution of all the organization's fund-raising campaigns.

The standing development committee has basic responsibility for overseeing and advising on the organization's fund-raising activities. Its main duties are to:

1. Set policies, priorities, and goals for fund-raising programs for the current fiscal year
2. Review the ongoing performance of each campaign
3. Review campaign achievement versus its objectives
4. Identify and rate all major prospects for support
5. Recruit key volunteer leadership and solicitors for the organization's fund-raising campaigns

Chairs of development committees (CDCs), like development directors, must resolve the various contributed-income needs of the organization without exhausting its base of support. The best CDCs are able to see the job in its entirety. They have broad vision. They don't fall in love with one fund-raising idea, campaign, or concept at the expense of the overall development effort.

My preferred CDC is a general managerial type with a strong marketing background. Ideally, the CDC is something of an alter ego for the development director. I have been my most successful when my CDCs and I shared the same fund-raising vision. In a sense, the best CDC is a leader whom a competent development director is able to lead. The CDC has clout within the community that the development director is unlikely to possess, while the latter has fund-raising knowledge that is probably outside the CDC's purview. The partnership between CDC and development director works best when the professional develops the ideas and then gains the agreement of the volunteer leader, who uses his clout to get cooperation from the board and other volunteer campaign leaders.

Non-profits with strong development operations also may have standing committees for ongoing fund-raising endeavors such as the annual fund. The chairs of these standing committees also sit on the standing development committee. Most of the members of these secondary committees will be trustees, but volunteer fund-raising leaders who are not trustees are also included.

The Team

To summarize, the two key members of the development team are the development director and the chair of the standing development committee. They, augmented by any consultants the organization engages, form an executive committee that is responsible for recruiting all other team members. The director of development hires and supervises any additional development department staff, all of whom are part of the team. The CDC recruits other development committee members, all of whom are part of the team.

These two groups, development department staff and development committee members, are the core of the team, its permanent members. From time to time others join the team when they are asked to carry out functions crucial to raising contributed income. They are the non-development department staff of the organization and the volunteer leaders and solicitors of fund-raising campaigns. The development team can be diagrammed as a group of concentric circles, with those closest to the center having the most direct and ongoing involvement.

Depending on the size and complexity of the organization, a number of staff members performing non-development functions can, from time to time, be thought of as part of the development team. These include members of the public relations,

accounting, and marketing departments, as well as the organization's executive director and, in the case of an arts organization, its creative director. The defining factor here is whether they are performing a function which supports the solicitation of funds. Obviously, the public relations department issues press releases and garners media coverage of fund-raising activities, and the accounting office keeps track of donations. If an organization has a marketing director charged with selling tickets, such as we did at the Cleveland Orchestra, that person can be a crucial member of the team, especially if you build a relationship based on goodwill and cooperation.

Gary Hanson, who is about the best marketing director I have ever known, came to the Cleveland Orchestra after I had worked with a few others in that post. All were fine professionals, but for one reason or another they and my department had not jelled. It wasn't long before Gary and I developed a comfortable working relationship and a genuine friendship. Remembering my experience with previous marketing directors and what I had heard over the years from many development professionals, I asked Gary, one day early in his tenure, "Why do you marketing people hate us development people?" Proof that I was not displaying my paranoia came in Gary's quick response. "Because you people promise the moon to donors and sponsors, and then you come to us demanding that we comply by providing tickets we could have sold or holding up printing schedules so that you can get a corporate logo on a poster or program."

He was right. That is exactly what I had done to his predecessors, to some degree, and was soon to do to him. However, now I understood that I was the one asking for a favor, and that I needed to include Gary on my development team. He probably never thought of himself as a "development team member," but I made sure that he was informed early and well about our activities, plans, and campaign needs. Gary became better able to anticipate what might be coming from us development people, and I was able to get stronger and quicker cooperation out of his marketing department.

Similarly, there are others in an organization from whom the development director will need to ask favors if a campaign is to run smoothly. The best way to get the cooperation of these colleagues is to think of them as members of the development team with a need to know just as legitimate as that of development department staff and development committee members.

The development team, then, is both a solid and a fluid group. At its center are the people who live and breathe fund-raising. They are the core of the team. Moving outward we find the organization staff members who perform functions that support fund-raising efforts, and the volunteer leadership who take responsibility for captaining campaigns. And finally, there are the volunteer solicitors who ask for the money. They are all part of the team, and they all contribute to the success of an organization's fund-raising efforts.

There we have it. To succeed in knowing your institution and its needs . . . building a team of motivated volunteers . . . and effectively soliciting donors takes *planning, persistent effort, and patience.* These are the keys to success in every aspect of fund-raising and development.

You will recall that in Chapter 1 we examined the *Nine Basic Truths of Fund-Raising.* In parting, why don't we make it "ten"? There is one more basic truth I'd like to leave you with. It comes in the form of this wise little jingle by Richard Armour:

Shake and shake the catsup bottle.
None will come, and then a lot'll.

Index

ORDER FORM

Please photocopy this page to order additional copies of *It's a Great Day to Fund-Raise!*

Yes, please send me:

QUANTITY

_____ *It's a Great Day to Fund-Raise!* by Tony Poderis. $35.00 <u>hardcover</u>. Plus $6 shipping and handling for one copy, $1.25 more for each additional copy. Ohio residents add 5.75% state sales tax to the retail cost of the books.

_____ *It's a Great Day to Fund-Raise!* by Tony Poderis. $22.95 <u>softcover</u>. Plus $5.50 shipping and handling for one copy, $1 more for each additional copy. Ohio residents add 5.75% state sales tax to the retail cost of the books.

For special rates for bulk orders, write FundAmerica Press at the address below.

☐ Check made payable to FundAmerica Press enclosed

Name _____

Street address _____
(No P.O. Box numbers, please; we ship UPS.)

City _____ State _____ Zip _____

Daytime phone no. _____

☐ Please send a gift copy of *It's a Great Day to Fund-Raise!* to:

Name _____

Street address _____
(No P.O. Box numbers, please; we ship UPS.)

City _____ State _____ Zip _____

Gift message to read: _____

_____

_____

Name _____

Street address _____
(No P.O. Box numbers, please; we ship UPS.)

City _____ State _____ Zip _____

Gift message to read: _____

_____

_____

Mail payment and order form to:
FundAmerica Press
2901 Istra Lane
Willoughby Hills, Ohio 44092